D1243995

This One's for the Working Mama

PERMISSION TO LIVE WITH YOUR SOUL ON FIRE

Katie T. Alexander

WESTBOW
PRESS®
A DIVISION OF THOMAS NELSON
& ZONDERVAN

WestBow Press books may be ordered through booksellers or by contacting:

WestBow Press
A Division of Thomas Nelson & Zondervan
1663 Liberty Drive
Bloomington, IN 47403
www.westbowpress.com
1 (866) 928-1240

ISBN: 978-1-9736-6402-4 (sc)
ISBN: 978-1-9736-6401-7 (hc)
ISBN: 978-1-9736-6403-1 (e)

Library of Congress Control Number: 2019906225

Print information available on the last page.

WestBow Press rev. date: 8/6/2019

For my girls, Ella and Meadow. May you never forget that your mama worked _and_ loved you big! You are my greatest accomplishment.

Contents

Introduction

Why I Wrote This Book

Writing a book is a funny process. It's not laugh out loud funny; it's peculiar and perplexing. The road is well mapped out for how authors come to be published and the gate is narrow. While many write, few get through the passage to hold a book in their hand. It all begins with the proposal. The first step in creating your proposal to agents and publishers is describing your credibility as an expert on the topic. How do you begin to define being an expert at working motherhood? If we are mamas and we work, aren't we all experts on that topic? Yes, the expert is every mom who's in the trenches of a nine-to-five job. The expert is you and it is I. I am no different than you, so please don't see my name on the cover of this book and believe that I am something more. I simply listened to the call God placed on my heart to put these words on a page.

I looked for a resource like this for years and kept coming up empty handed. I needed to read that someone else fed their kids frozen waffles in the car on the ride to school and on occasion had to wear a bathing suit as underwear because laundry was overdue. My soul yearned to hear that my kids would not need therapy because I couldn't be their class mom or go on every field trip. Or that someone else felt the struggle of their phone being the constant guest at their play dates or family dinners. More than all of that, I really needed encouragement and truth that could set my guilty heart free, because let's be honest, the mom guilt struggle is real.

I think you picked up this book because you can relate with at least one of those needs and you long for something, whether it's peace, order in the chaos, joy for the journey, or just one person who gets it. I hope to be that person for you—a typical woman working her way through a job, life, and parenting, trying to keep it all together. Through all of these ups and downs of motherhood, there is one constant for me. My hope is found in the Lord, at the feet of Jesus. If you don't know that hope and you don't know that Savior, I pray you don't put the book down on the assumption that we can't relate. Keep reading, and just maybe you will find your hope. If you do know Him (at least on some level), my prayer over this book is that through my transparency, my vulnerability, and my story you find the encouragement and strength to pull yourself out of the trenches and ready yourself for a new day, a new battle, and a victory that can be found in only One.

Your path shouldn't be guilt-ridden just because you work, even if that choice differs from your mom's, your sister's, or your friends'. I could tell you to drop this guilt for being a working mama, but hearing me (or anyone else) say this over and over is not going to do you a bit of good when you are faced with one of those mommy failure moments. So rather than tell you to feel something different, I plan to *show* you how I found freedom and peace in my choices. With the right tools, I believe you can too because the One I turn to isn't a guilt maker; He's a grace giver.

I am not a theologian or a biblical expert. I am just a regular mom who loves Jesus, her husband, and her kids. I balance all of those commitments with a job outside the home in corporate America. Through this book, I am also the woman in your Bible study group who shows up and pours out her soul without fear of judgment. I am the one who will be at your house late in the evening in pajamas and sit next to you on the couch as you digest the words on the page. I'm the friend you can invite to your favorite coffee shop as you sip on your drink of choice. And as you hold this book in your hands, I hope that you envision I am sitting across from you because we are in this together. This is not just about my journey.

I expect as you read some of my story and tips for letting go and letting God work, there will be laughs and possibly tears because my story was not always easy or perfect, but the One who is perfect carried me when I needed it most. The truth is, not every day felt like a dream, not every step in my career felt fulfilling or directed, and some days I would retreat to my closet, sit in the quiet stillness of that private place and cry. There isn't one defining moment that kept me returning here, it was a series of events and influences that unleashed the tears. I would cry because the guilt got the best of me or I started to believe a narrative that said I failed at either my job or my home. I caved to the lie that being a working mother was a selfish choice and I began to question every decision that led me there. There are days where I still need this escape, to feel the carpet beneath my knees as I surrender to the Lord. But now, these trips to my closet look a bit different because I have the right tools to find rest when my soul is weary.

I made a bold promise on the cover that this book would give you permission to live with a soul on fire. I'm confident this is attainable if you can lean into grace, change your thinking and spend a little time in your closet... or wherever you pray. If you're skeptical and don't believe me, at least I've got you reading. That's a great place to start. The pages of this book are intended to serve as a way to balance all the guilt producing lies with truth grounded in God's Word. They're a high five for hanging in there. They're a place for community with someone who understands your struggles and has shared the trenches of working mama parenting. Together we will step into the permission to embrace freedom from guilt. But first, I feel it is important to start by sharing with you my road to becoming a mother—a working mother.

Chapter 1

For the New Mama: The Road to Motherhood

*Then you will experience God's peace, which exceeds
anything we can understand. His peace will guard your
hearts and minds as you live in Christ Jesus.*
Philippians 4:7

I always envy people who talk about their passion for running. The way an avid runner describes picking up speed and falling into deep thought while feeling the pavement pound under their feet sounds like a liberating experience. Many of my friends who are runners describe this as the time when they are closest to God. They push out the thoughts that keep their minds racing, focus on their breathing, and find a rhythm that allows them a clear head to start dialoguing with the Lord.

In the fall of my senior year of college, I decided I needed to know what this was all about. I purchased my first pair of running shoes and loaded my iPod up with music. I mapped out a single mile path on campus that was well-lit at night. Then one evening, I just walked out and started to run. I didn't get very far before I was short of breath and started to feel a pain in my side. I had never trained, nor had I properly paced myself. I just set out and ran as fast as I could. I did this same routine for several days in a row, never finding that "runner's zone" I had heard so much about. I also failed to connect with Jesus because my time was spent breathing so deeply, focusing on the countdown to the finish, and thinking I may in fact meet the good Lord before the mile was up!

It was with this same head-on force that I approached the road to becoming a mom. I was twenty-two years old and married two years when we decided to start a family. Two years into my career, I felt like it was a comfortable time to embark into motherhood. I never thought for a minute about giving up my job; it just seemed like we could fit all these pieces together. The only thing I was lacking to complete my perfect picture of being a working mom was the baby. After six months with no success, I applied the same urgency with which I had tackled running that fall of my senior year to getting myself into a fertility clinic as soon as possible. In my first round of testing with the physician, we had a humbling and heart-stopping conversation about the path I would need to take to get pregnant. The doctor diagnosed me with polycystic ovarian syndrome (PCOS), which seemed like a lot of fancy words to say that this was not going to be a sprint but a marathon. According to research conducted by the Mayo Clinic, PCOS is a hormone disorder with an unknown cause that inhibits maturation of follicles in the ovaries and regular ovulation. Some of the symptoms were present as far back as I could remember: irregular menstrual cycles, difficulty losing weight, and acne that began early in my youth and continued well into my adult years. Another common symptom that I praise Jesus I was spared is excess facial hair. With all of those other things going for me, the last thing I needed was a beard! With a diagnosis rooted in an "unknown cause," I would have to train my brain to think differently and understand that this journey to parenting was as much out of my control as the waves and the tide.

Every single day after that, when I encountered people who were pregnant, it felt like a little piece of me was breaking. During my marathon of fertility treatments, which included medications, diagnostic tests, ultrasounds, and countless specialist visits, I was undergoing a different kind of training as well—one of the heart. The twenty-three months I spent working with my doctor and waiting for good news to appear on the ultrasound screens taught me so much about my faith. This battle with infertility seemed like the first real struggle I had encountered that my parents, my spouse, or I could not fix. I had to arrive at a point where I surrendered this part of my future completely to the Lord, but this surrender did not come easily.

One day in August of 2007, after nearly two years of treatments, I was starting the last round of fertility medicine my doctor would prescribe before we moved to more serious options. I collapsed to my knees on the hardwood floor of our master bedroom with salty tears streaming down my face. I clenched the fertility pills firmly in my hand as I cried out, "Why Lord? Why is it this path for me? Why couldn't this just be spontaneous and easy like it is for so many others?"

Most of my friends could date back their conceptions with romantic stories, while mine was taking place in a sterile room with white walls and stirrup covers that resembled mauve oven mitts your grandmother would knit. Rather than wining, dining, and romancing, our fertility specialist sat us down at a table before the procedure and drew a diagram of all the lady parts to describe the sperm as a tiny car driving through the vagina to find the garage in the follicle. From that moment on, all that I could envision was a Volkswagen Beetle in my abdomen. This was not how I dreamed pregnancy happened. All of the failed medication and unsuccessful procedures had started to steal my joy.

Six rounds of fertility medication with no change in the ultrasound screen resulted in a belief that God wasn't listening to my cries. During that period of doubt, I exhausted every bit of my own strength, and I was losing hope. I was ready to buy a two-seater convertible and move to a one-bedroom high rise in the city, because when I do pity party, I do it big! This irrational and hopeless behavior erupted because I had shifted my focus from God's will to my own.

I remember sitting at the table of my weekly Bible study group in the midst of this battle and sharing with the group through tears that I was not going to keep going. I was worn out physically and emotionally. I was ready to be done. I told these ladies that I had given up, I no longer needed to have a baby. They could see right through this lie, and one of them started to press and ask me questions. Why the change of heart? What happened? I explained that the fertility medication had produced a cyst that needed an immediate operation that would set everything back months. I had run into my fertility doctor in the parking garage at work and was so discouraged by the timeline he had laid out for the surgery and recovery that was necessary before we could resume treatments. He explained we would add three months for recovery before we could start back at square one.

Through this story, the inquiring woman, Debbie, could see the hand of God, so she took me firmly (and lovingly) by the shoulders and made her eyes match mine. She spoke these words that delved deep into my soul and that I will never forget. She said, "Katie, are you telling me that in your time of doubt and uncertainty, God places your fertility doctor in your parking garage to give you all the answers to your many questions and this is still not enough confirmation that you are on the right path?" Sometimes I just need to be smacked on the head, and that is exactly what Debbie did for me that day.

If we can look up from all the things we think we know and take a minute to pause our own plans, we may just find that God is smacking us on our heads at this very moment with something pivotal and monumental for our lives. We can determine our own way out of circumstances that may be the wrong way when the right path, the one made straight by leaning not on our own understanding, is in front of us in our work parking garages.

Debbie's gentle reprimand woke me up and helped me to stay the path. I had the procedure, and four months later I completed the last round of fertility medication. On August 17, 2007, God chose to answer my call for a baby in the middle of the Caribbean. I was fourteen days post fertility procedure on board a cruise with two pregnancy tests packed in my luggage. My husband stood in the doorway of our tiny cruise cabin bathroom as I took this test like so many before, but we had a new kind of hope. After taking nearly twenty pregnancy tests with negative results over the course of two years, my eyes could barely focus on the dark blue plus sign. Fourteen days after I kneeled in my bedroom with salty tears and surrendered my questions and doubts to God, He granted me the desire I had been longing for: I was pregnant. I spent eighteen dollars on a two-minute phone call to let my mom know, and then we sprinted down the hall to share the news with my in-laws, who were on board with us. Just for safe measures, I took seven more pregnancy tests that week that we picked up on port in Mexico, and each one kept confirming our news.

While being a mother was something I knew God had called me to in this life, the experience of getting there reminded me that the true prize is dwelling with Him in eternity. The race toward motherhood was one of testing my endurance and perseverance in trusting in Him no matter what the outcome. It seems I encounter someone almost every week that battles infertility on some level. My heart aches with every story because my human mind tells me it shouldn't be this way. We were designed to reproduce, to carry babies in our womb, to be mothers. The Spirit in me, however, reminds me that God's timing is best and His plan is greater and He will make a way.

If you are the reader who is walking through this battle at this very minute, I'm so thankful you found this. I hope that reading about a little piece of my struggle brings you encouragement and hope, because hope was the only thing I could cling to. Don't trade your sedan in for a two-seater car on impulse, because God may be planning something really big right up ahead if you can just let Him direct your path. In my fertility battle I realized one big thing about our God: He does not give us a desire that He cannot fulfill. I knew that God had planted this longing in me to be a mother, and even if I wasn't sure how He was going to fulfill that, I found comfort in knowing that He absolutely would. There was no obstacle to motherhood that was too great for Him.

I thought the battle with infertility was going to be one of my greatest tests of faith, until I encountered the challenges of motherhood. The struggles with infertility were internal battles of wrestling with my own mind and emotions, but I quickly learned that the pressures of motherhood are both external and internal. Whether you ask for it or not, you will get more advice than you can possibly process. This begins almost immediately, when it's time to discuss your intent to work or stay home and how you will feed your child.

After we had a positive pregnancy test and cleared some of the hurdles of the first trimester, I dealt with the internal debate of when to tell my boss. I had no reason to believe it would be greeted with anything but congratulations, but it was still a nerve-racking decision. I had responsibilities at my job that no one else knew how to perform, and even though pregnancy is a very normal thing in the lives of women, I didn't know how entering into motherhood would affect your work. I finally built up enough courage around eleven weeks to enter her office for my regularly scheduled one-on-one meeting. With my heart racing a little faster than normal, I sat down and pulled out my agenda for the meeting. As I stared at the paper, I blurted out "I'm pregnant" before we even exchanged introductions. After the words were out, it was like the pressure left the room, and I looked up and my eyes met hers. Her reaction was loving and warm, and her response was completely unexpected. She said, "Katie, I've known for two weeks." No one had told her, and she hadn't snuck into my medical record. She had formed her own conclusion based on my routine restroom usage, my change in eating habits, and the changes in my appearance, like a breakout of acne and a little extra cushion in the midsection. It was an absolute relief to have this secret out in the open, but I hadn't expected her follow-up question: "Are you going to keep working or stay home after you have the baby?" I had not given any thought to an option other than continuing in my job. I was twenty-five years old, and that seemed like a young age to stop the climb up the career ladder that I had just begun.

My boss wasn't the last person to ask me this question. People asked me more times than I could count. I felt the answer was obvious until I was reminded there is a great big world out there of women who do not work and probably have really good reasons for choosing that. At first this question made me aggravated. Then the aggravation turned to guilt because sometimes the response I received was rooted in judgment. On occasion someone would utter a statement like, "I just don't know how anyone can leave their baby," not giving thought to what power their words had over my new mama mind. These statements would breed guilt, and from guilt would come apologetic explanations like, "But I have to work." We are going to tackle this topic in greater detail in Chapter 4, but for now I'll leave you with knowing that if you got this question repeatedly, you are not alone. And I'm going to show you how God gives us freedom to be confident in our decision and unapologetic in our answer later.

Those apologies we feel we owe the world for making our own paths into motherhood are the lies I hope to address over and over again in the pages of this book. The lies are not reserved for fertility battles or breastfeeding challenges; those are just the beginning of a lifetime of pressures that stem from standards set by the world around you. I hope to show you that we can find freedom in this life to live, parent, and work in a way that we don't owe an explanation or justification to anyone other than God. Like most big decisions in my life, I prayed over the decision of being a working mom. I prayed that God would give me peace with my decision and confirmation that this path was best for our family. And every day He answered that prayer with peace.

On April 19, 2008, I welcomed the most anticipated, prayed-for, and cherished little one who had the sweetest baby smell and her daddy's long brown eyelashes. The minute she entered the world I scooped her up in my arms and held her tight. Her tiny heartbeat and each little breath mesmerized me. This was the fulfillment of God's promise that He had a plan for me. Ella Marie was beautifully knit together in my womb. The very sight of her unlocked a love I didn't know existed for another person. In the blink of an eye, I was suddenly responsible for this little life, and as much as I wanted to soak in the moment, there was no denying that the pressure to be a certain type of mom began when they placed her in my arms for the first time.

It only took about eight minutes of her life for this mama to get hit by the humbling mom topic of breastfeeding. I'm going to get real here for a minute and tell you that before giving birth, I judged the you-know-what out of people who didn't breastfeed. Leading up to my own experience of motherhood, I sat in the driver's seat of the judging bus with the mindset that God created us with the ability to breastfeed and so that was what we as women needed to do. I'm sure I came to this strong opinion by way of some of my parenting books, blogs, and mommy message boards, but whatever the origin, the feeling was rooted and solidified.

I remember them handing me Ella after she had been cleaned up and swaddled tightly in a blanket like a little burrito. I held her as she was starting to open her little eyes and take in her new world and tried to take it all in and commit it to memory. In the midst of that baby gazing session, I remember the nurse telling me to just let her root for the breast and the rest would come naturally. I thought we were doing just fine and that I was quickly going to be the breastfeeding champion of Tampa, but twenty-four hours later, we learned she wasn't getting anything and had only dry diapers.

The pediatrician was a little alarmed by this and called in the lactation consultant. From what I knew of this role, I believed most lactation consultants had a calling to encourage moms who were struggling by offering support and being their cheerleader. The woman who entered my room was just a few yards shy of this calling. Without much of an introduction, she firmly grabbed my breast and the back of my baby's head and brought the two together in such a force that had I not been restrained by the Boppy pillow she may have been dodging a slap. I tried to relax and accept that she was the expert and let her do her thing. Fifteen minutes passed, during which my baby screamed nonstop. The stress of these fifteen minutes had cumulated in my own tears flowing, and then the most baffling thing happened—the consultant abruptly left the room. On her way out the door she said over her shoulder that she would be back to try again later. *Please no!* I thought. *Lock the doors and keep her away from my lady parts and my baby!*

I built a soap box as a result of this experience, and before I mount it, I would like to preface it by saying I'm sure lactation consultants the world over are not all like this one. There's plenty of evidence about the breast being best for baby, and I still believe it is a beautiful, God-given way to bond and nurture your offspring, so please don't send hate mail! But it was not for me.

We introduced a bottle at thirty-two hours because of the concern for nutrients, and with that bottle came the most overwhelming feeling of failure I'd ever met in my life. I'd built the belief that being a mom and doing it well meant providing by breastfeeding. The repercussions of all of my own judging came at me in ten-foot waves of disappointment and depression. Looking back on that now, I am able to see that all of this judgment I felt was false. Lies! For every lactation consultant who comes into a postpartum room to tell the importance of breastfeeding, I believe there should be a grace consultant as well. Someone who comes in and says, "Mama, your body is a mess, your hormones are out of whack, your mind is racing with the new responsibilities of this little baby, and your bladder may never be the same. Give yourself some room for grace. Love your baby and love yourself enough to sleep when you need it, and don't give into the pressures of the books or blogs or mommy groups. You will do this the way that is best for you and your baby, and that will be good enough." To hear those words would have saved me from weeks of continuing to fight and force this breastfeeding thing to work when really all my baby girl wanted was some food and she didn't care which method delivered it, as long as it was quick!

The same lesson I learned of leaning into God's grace for the fertility battle came back in neon lights with this new struggle. The breastfeeding drama taught me that the first rule of approaching motherhood is to never look at it as only having one path or one solution. I believed this was the only way to provide for your baby, and I reasoned that if I was not able to succeed at this then I must have been failing. But God reminded me there's always room for grace, for the scenario that doesn't fit the textbook. I think back on those two days in the hospital after Ella was born and I wish somebody, anybody, would have just looked me in the eye and said it was my choice and the pressure I felt to do this thing and do it perfectly was a lie I was going to face time and time again.

Finally, four weeks into this battle of nursing, pumping, and formula feeding that left me constantly defeated and frustrated, I stopped the madness. I looked at it as accepting defeat and decided to focus on other ways to bond with the baby. I was so wrong to think this way. Do you know what came as a result of this decision that felt riddled with failure? We were both better off. I stopped dreading feeding time. I embraced the snuggles and the bottle, which allowed Daddy to participate and give me time for a shower or quick nap. All of us were much happier. If I am being perfectly honest with you (and myself), I knew in the hospital on day two that this wasn't going to work, but I thought I needed someone's approval to stop. Looking back on this experience I see it was a foreshadowing of a lifetime of choosing between what others tell me is best and what is God's best. I was not throwing in a towel of defeat or failing this mom duty. God was simply choosing to lead me down a different path.

Working mamas have one of the greatest challenges when it comes breastfeeding. Regardless of how natural the act of nursing is, returning to work adds so many layers of complexity. You have to remember your pump and all its parts each day, store the milk, find the time and the place to do it, and keep it as discrete as possible from your male coworkers. In my office I always felt for the breastfeeding mama who had to explain to her boss (sometimes a male) every time she needed to take a milk break. You have to store your supply in the communal fridge next to people's coffee creamer and get very little privacy over the fact that you are lactating.

I've worked with so many women who can't keep this up, lose milk production, or can't get their babies to accept the bottle, and the result is many tears for everyone. The tears flow because we have bought into the lie that if we do not provide for our babies in this way we are somehow failing them. The pressure can be stronger when you are a working mom because you need to prove to yourself and your baby that you are doing everything you can for them. We give far too much authority over our lives to lactation consultants, friends, or "experts" who tells us this is the *only* way to adequately provide. Why is one mom's decision for herself and her baby anybody else's business? I was the mom in the Mommy and Me group who was shaking up the formula bottle while the rest of them threw on their hooter hiders and went to their business. I am here to tell you that I survived being odd woman out and even learned to let the few judgmental glances roll off my back. After beating myself up over this for long enough, I chose to bring it to God in prayer and let Him take the guilt and bring me peace with my decision. If you do you with prayerful consideration, you can't go wrong!

We live in a time in which we take on so much control and have a world of information at our fingertips. We love to research things to death. There's more information available to us than ever before, but so much of it is diluted in opinion. One thing this whole experience has taught me is that there is still only one truth in the entire world that we can turn to as a resource, and that is God's Word. While you may not find explicit instructions for breastfeeding in the gospel, what you will find is confirmation that God's best for your life is a life lived in His will. The only way to get there is by putting Him at the center.

The way I came to my final decision to allow this breastfeeding adventure to come to an end was through prayer. I prayed God would give me confirmation that it was okay for Ella if I stopped. His answer came in the most obvious and welcome way: peace. I found peace with my decision, and He continued to confirm it as I was able to find a new level of joy in my early days as a mama. It was the same peace God had brought me after seeing my fertility specialist in the parking garage, the same peace that would carry me through the race to pregnancy and the goal line of birth, and the same peace I would come to rely on to guide me through the path of motherhood as a working mama.

Whether you are in a stage of motherhood of conceiving and breastfeeding, selecting the right preschool, raising a teenager, or helping your nearly adult child make a decision on a college, chances are you feel uncertainty about the path before you. There may be so many voices around you attempting to influence your decisions on the next step for your career or parenting that it has become difficult to weed through the noise to find the truth. The uncertainties are limiting you from living with your soul on fire, and instead your soul is confused and tormented. If you're like me, you rise daily with desperation to fill a constant longing in your soul and find a path to freedom from guilt over all the decisions of motherhood. So how do we practically get there?

Let me ask you right now, what was the best day of your life? What day can you point to when all your senses let you know you were really living? I have a couple. I've talked about one of them in my story of the day Ella entered the world. If I could bottle the joy and excitement of that day and sprinkle a little on each day forward I certainly would, but through this journey God is continuously showing me there is another way to live your best. My soul was created to long for nourishment and vivacious living. If I want to find food, living water, and ignition for the fire, I must daily return to the source. We don't have to guess what the source is. In John 6:51, Jesus tells us, "I am the living bread that came down from heaven. Anyone who eats this bread will live forever, and this bread, which I will offer so the world may live, is my flesh." Jesus is the bread of life. But how do we find Him, since we do not live in a time when the human presence of Jesus walks the earth? The Bible says in John 1:1, "In the beginning the Word already existed, the Word was with God and the Word was God." We have Him right at our fingertips in the physical presence of the Bible.

I believe that we, as working moms, are trying to live a life that checks the boxes of success, trying to live right, serve others, and do our very best. If we look to the world to define success for us, it tells us conflicting messages that will leave us chasing dreams and coming up empty. It tells us to work longer hours, put our jobs first, and strive for better titles, more money, and higher status. And every single one of these choices and sacrifices will leave you with a deeper hunger, a deeper thirst, and flat-out exhaustion. Ladies, if you want living bread, the bread that gives life to your spirit in a way that has lasting power, look no further than the Word of God. In my introduction I promised a pathway to freedom, and this is day one, where we begin. Just like my journey to motherhood wasn't a sprint but a marathon, getting to know God takes time. According to most research, it takes twenty-eight days to form a habit. I am challenging you to spend the next thirty-one days with me as we commit to beginning our day with daily bread.

Chapter 1 Application
The Nourishment Commitment

I, _____, commit to myself and to God to spend thirty-one days drawing my nourishment from the Living Bread. I will make time each day to open my Bible and be in the Word. This day, _____, is day one.

Don't commit to this plan as a checklist. I urge you to make it so much more! This is the beginning of a life well lived. Join me as we work through the book of Proverbs in the Bible together. The purpose of the Proverbs is to teach people to live disciplined and successful lives. This is a biblical definition of the success we can strive for without guilt. The Proverbs are quick instructions defining the difference between right and wrong, fair and just. It is an instruction manual and a path to living fully. Just a few minutes of each day can clear up confusion and put you on a new path to success, one that is in line with God's will for your life.

Nourishment Challenge lived out:

✓ Read one chapter of Proverbs a day for thirty-one days. You can use a Bible application or your Bible. I encourage a physical Bible, but I know if you're trying to do this on a busy day your phone may be your best option. If that's the case, keep a notebook close by to jot down the things you want to remember. Any version of the Bible is great. I default to the New Living Translation.

✓ Use a pencil, pen, or highlighter and identify truths you need as reminders in your life.

✓ Choose one truth to put into application in your life. Either commit it to memory, pray it over a specific challenge you are facing, or journal your current situation with that truth in mind.

✓ Follow along with the Nourishment Challenge devotions on This One's for the Working Mama Podcast, episodes 1-31 on iTunes and Spotify.

Chapter 2

The Home Front: Lessons I Learned from My Mama

Direct your children onto the right path, and
when they are old they will not leave it,
Proverbs 22:6

Hi, I'm Katie, and I am a perfection-aholic. I could start this chapter off by telling you that perfection is unattainable and pretend like there is enough power in those words to hit our reset buttons. I could urge you to start new with room for error, grace for yourself, and dependence on the unending mercies found in the Lord. But I know that those words are not enough to change my thinking, so I'm going to assume that they also won't be enough for those of you who are likewise struggling with perfectionism.

No scholar or author is going to tell me to drop the desire for perfection and have it make a lasting impact because everywhere I look I am bombarded by this standard. Social media would not have skyrocketed to its popularity if we were not a society focused on the idea of perfection. When is the last time you scrolled your feed and saw photo after photo of real life, real mess, and captions like "I just fought with my husband, yelled at my kids, wanted to kick my dog, and it's not even 9 A.M. yet"? I'll be honest, because that's what this journey is about, you won't see it on my feed either. We carefully craft our photo scenes, we take several shots to get the right one, we frame in the one spot without a mess, we yell at our kids to smile, and we crop and edit to meet our standards. I don't live life through the lens of my social media account, but I constantly strive to achieve this idea of perfection in all aspects of my life. The result is a continuous shortcoming because being perfect is not attainable. There is no filter for life itself. I chase my tail, run in circles, and get to the point of total body, mind, and spirit exhaustion for which there is only one cure. I escape to my closet and sit on the floor in the dark, hug my knees close to my chest, and have a little moment that starts as a pity party and ends with the Lord. My mom taught me that!

Motherhood is defined by so many factors. Most of the time, whether conscious or subconscious, it starts with our own moms. Whether the mothering you received was good, bad, or nonexistent, it contributes to the way you define yourself as a mother. My mom is a unique woman. Growing up, she mothered the way Jesus would command, and she did it with grace and poise. The seemingly effortless way that she was a wife and a mother gave me this idea that perfection was something that was attainable. This is a woman who always begins her day with the Lord, no matter what. Hours before our little eyes even opened in the morning, she would be on her knees, Bible open, in the stillness of His presence. She was the type of mom who had a hot breakfast on the table, the house spotless before dawn, and our lunches packed with crusts cut off the bread and special notes tucked inside.

My mom didn't do this parenting thing alone, though. My dad was also pretty great. My dad brought the laughter and the fun and often left my mom praying for a sense of humor so that she could keep up with his antics. In my high school years, my dad started to pack my lunch, and every day was an adventure. He went to one of those photo booths in the mall and had little stickers made of his face. He bought me a dozen vintage metal lunch boxes, and in each one he inscribed, "This is my dad. He packs my lunch every day," above those little stickers of his face. People would crowd around our lunch table to see what surprise was in store. One day, he asked what I wanted packed, and I flippantly said, "One of everything." I opened my lunch box the next day to find literally one of every item in our pantry individually packed in its own Ziploc bag. There was a twenty-dollar bill taped to the bottom because he realized that one peanut, one cheerio, one Oreo, one cracker, one grape, and one pretzel would not be a filling lunch.

My dad was incredibly hands-on and present when he could be, but he also worked long hours so that my mom could stay home with us in our early years. We never felt like we were lacking because on my dad's late nights, my mom would make dinner, pack it picnic style, and take us up to his work to eat with him. I remember these dinner visits as some of my favorite moments. I can still picture the brown Pyrex dish my mom used to hold his meal and how he would always make us laugh as we ate with him and spun around in the conference room chairs. The fact that he didn't get home until long past our bedtime those nights was lost on us because we cherished those adventures to his workplace and dinners around his conference room table.

When my mom was in the trenches of parenting while my dad was busy at work, she rarely got mad, never had a temper, and never used a bad word (Okay, we've heard her say exactly five in our entire lifetimes, and I can recount each time with so much laughter because it was completely out of character). When we had pushed her buttons or she'd finally had enough, she would quietly escape to her room, enter her closet, and from her knees reach out to God for renewal and nourishment for her soul.

God began to alter the path for my mom's life when my dad had a major career shift and our family had to relocate a couple hours south of our home. The move would require my mom to take a job with my dad's company because cost of living was higher and they were starting to think about things like college funds and weddings. This move impacted me because even though it was only about a two-hour drive, it seemed to my twelve-year-old brain like we were moving to a different solar system. I had only ever lived in one town and gone to school with the friends I had since first grade. All of that was an immense amount of change to deal with, but the biggest part of this transition was that I would learn to view my mom in a new light, as a working mama.

With all the same grace, poise, and balance with which she had tackled being a stay-at-home mom, she rocked the working mom role too. I was a pre-teen, starting to see things in a different way as I was building my own goals and dreams. Watching my mom start at the very bottom in their company and build her way to the top sparked something in me. I wanted to be like her in this new way. In a mostly male-dominated field, my mom managed to be one of the top 100 best sales professionals in the country. Her career path provided confirmation that it was good to dream big and want this type of accomplishment for my own life.

I felt compelled to share a bit of my mom's story because maybe you had to go back to work after a season of being home with your kids. Perhaps that decision was so difficult at the time or you are walking in it right now. I believe that no matter when we have to make this decision to be a mom who works, all the questions, anxieties, and fears about what that may hold are the same. Will our kids be okay? Will we be able to balance it all? Can I really have a thriving career and fulfilled family? While I cherish those early days with my mom at home, the years she went back to work were something that molded and shaped the trajectory of my life so much more than my first twelve years when our routine was predictable and she was PTA mom.

Adjusting to this new normal of having a mom who worked outside the home was challenging for all of us. My mom had to learn a new normal and reconstruct her ideas of the perfect home. Sometimes laundry had to be dropped off at the cleaner's to keep up, and there was a season when she had to bring in a cleaning service. There were weeks when we ate more takeout than usual. However, none of these adjustments scarred my childhood or altered the dynamic of our family. In fact, they made it better. My mom's ability to adapt to the changes and implement new systems allowed us to continue to make time for the things that mattered most.

Perfection is obviously unattainable and in contrast to the theme of this book. As perfect as my mom continues to appear, she has made so much room in her life for the Lord and His mercies to rain new every morning. My mom set a standard of motherhood so incredibly off the charts that I'm positive I could never reach it. When you grow up under this type of parenting, it can impact your impression of how your own role of motherhood will look. My mom made it look so effortless that I thought one day you have a baby and it all just flows. I believed that the house stayed clean, the kids would always be well dressed and fed, I would maintain my figure and appearance, and dinner would somehow magically appear on the table at 6 P.M. Then I had my first baby and realized that one seven-pound, ten-ounce little human had the ability to pick up the snow globe that contained my tidy little life and shake it with impeccable force.

Looking back on my years growing up at home, I wish my mom would have just cracked and told me, "This mom thing is so hard." I wish her private moments with the Lord in her closet were lived more publicly in front of my brother and myself. Seeing frustrations lived out would have given me the permission I need to feel normal when I have moments of my own. Instead, I have to learn this in the trenches of motherhood as I tackle battle after battle and redefine my own idea of perfection. I think we all are perfectionists on some level. If we are created in the image of our perfect Father, it is no surprise that we would long to be more like Him.

From the beginning of humanity, the Garden of Eden was intended to be a place of ultimate perfection. Mankind was permitted to live and enjoy this scene until we went and messed it up. It is ingrained in our human nature from our very first ancestors that we should long for a perfect home, and that is how God always intended it to be. Until we are face-to-face with Jesus and allowed to re-enter that garden, we have to learn to find "good enough" here on earth. I will always strive for some idea of perfect, but I am learning to cover that idea in the knowledge that I will never be perfect this side of heaven. I'm redefining what an attainable "good enough" can look like in my own life and realizing that this desire to be perfect is strangling my soul, crippling my testimony, and ruining this life.

As a working mama, your time will always be a juggling act, and there is potential to feel a hundred steps behind. If your goal for picking up this book was to find hope and refreshment for your soul, bringing some order into your home and routine is a great place to start. You can find your garden here on earth, whether it's a mansion or a humble apartment. The condition of your physical building does not define your home. The tone you set, the way you personalize it, and the way you make space in it for the ones you love is how you build your sanctuary.

Have you ever met a person who says, "I just hate when my house is clean," or "I can't stand when my schedule is laid out and my week is organized"? Many people, myself included, use the excuse that we don't have time for that level of organization. The reality is, we all have the same time in a day but we get caught up letting our circumstances dictate and derail how we use it. Creating a routine of just a few tasks you complete each day can stop the madness of things piling up and the feeling that you are a prisoner to your mess. You can get control of your house, schedule, chores, and thoughts by putting some practical applications in place. Whether you implement all of the following or just a few, I'm confident you will find this brings some balance to your crazy, chaotic, and precious life. You can enjoy living more of it in the moment rather than watching it pass you by from your kitchen sink or laundry room after a long day at work. Here are a few of my favorite tips—consider them lessons learned in the trenches—for tackling your home front as you balance it with your work life:

Chapter 2 Application
Creating order

- **Make your bed every day.** My mom made her bed every day for as long as I can remember. She passed this on to us, and it was one of the few chores that were non-negotiable. When I got into my own home I rebelled. This was, at the time, my least favorite chore. I'm certain my bed and the fifteen throw pillows I had accumulated didn't see "made form" for nearly five years. One day, I just did it. I repurposed most of the throw pillows and simplified it to one quilt, the pillows we slept with, and two king pillows with shams and have kept it that way. We don't even use a top sheet. It takes us less than a minute each morning to throw this together, and if you get your spouse or kid to help, it cuts the time in half.

  The repetition of this daily chore has created a habit that isn't just about appearances, it serves me. I walk into my master bedroom at least a dozen times, but that last trek in at the end of the night is when it matters the most. That's when I feel the weight of a thousand things that passed through my mind in the last twelve hours about to cripple me into slumber. There is nothing like falling into that made bed. The hospitality industry is on to something with the midday cleaning and evening turndowns. It welcomes you in. Now that my kids are old enough to at least give it their best try, this is the first item on their chore chart. After several years of putting this habit into practice, on the rare occasion when I have to run out the door without doing this, I'll come home to notice my husband has done it because even he has come to appreciate it!

- **Clean up after your kids every day.** This probably seems excessive, and you might be thinking, "Shouldn't the kids clean up their own mess?" I think we need to pause and remember that our kids are not born with an innate ability to tidy up; they are looking to us to set that example and teach them. I don't allow my kids to just sit by and watch me clean up their mess. If they are home I engage them in the cleanup so that they can learn how to put things away.

Countless psychological studies and books have been compiled about a child's need for order and structure. When you minimize their options and create separation between toys, they can see clearly what they want to play with and are far more likely to keep all of the castle figures or princesses together in the same container. In our current house I finally built the playroom of my dreams. The kids think it's pretty cool, but what does that matter? I am obsessed! Each type of activity is separated in its own labeled storage bin. While my youngest can't read the labels yet, she starts each day fresh and knows which bins which toys belong to.

Chances are, if you are working outside the home, Monday through Friday your kids are spending a large part of their day in school or childcare. The time spent at home in their little sanctuary is probably limited comparatively. It always amazes me how much mess my kids can make when on average they only spend three hours of their day at home awake. If I were to let this mess accumulate for the five working days, by the time we got to the weekend we would have to use shovels to dig our way through the piles of toys, princess costumes, and Barbie shoes. Saturday morning would roll around, and instead of entering the playroom, my kids would be turned off by the clutter and want to grab an iPad and sit on the couch. Some nights I am just too tired to straighten up. I pass by and look the other direction or physically kick items back into the playroom that have made their way to the hallway. I don't beat myself up over this, but I do know that those items will be double or triple the amount the next day. If I don't want to spend my entire weekend cleaning up after my kids and my family, I need to make some adjustments that begin during the week.

- **Don't spend your weekends on the minutia.** On average, we work five days a week, eight to ten hours a day, just to arrive at that splendor that is the weekend. For years—and I mean like thirteen years too many—we let the laundry pile up for Saturday washing and drying and Sunday folding. We take two or three hours to grocery shop and put things away, resulting in a fridge cleanout and pantry dump. Then, every other weekend, we can't stand the dog hair tumbleweeds or spotted shower glass one minute longer and it becomes a half-day project to whip the house in order. All the while the kids are just waiting for the fun to begin. They want our time and attention, even if it's something as simple as playing Play-Doh or going to the community pool.

  For far too long we have wasted time during these precious weekends with chores. I wrestled with this off and on and figured there had to be some solution. We were not rolling in dough by any means. We were both early in our careers when we had Ella, twenty-five years old and with two car payments, a mortgage, and some revolving expenses. But I started asking around to friends with cleaning services and found a woman who was willing to do just the things I needed for $65 a session. This was a time in my life when money was my greatest source of stress, but I determined enough was enough. I went back through the budget and realized if I could just make a few adjustments by way of giving up two lunches out a month and one trip to Target, I could swing this. I hired this woman, Helen, and she changed my life by coming once a month. This wasn't happenstance; it was an answer to prayer. I prayed God would make a way to get back family time, and He delivered someone who was so efficient and thorough that I didn't even miss the "deep clean" every other week. I could straighten up during the week and allow the big stuff to wait for the third Tuesday. Having someone scrub the floors, wipe the baseboards, deep clean the bathrooms, and dust made the time between her visits that much easier.

  To stretch out my once-a-month cleaning, I made it easy to clean up in between sessions. I made the switch to cleaning products that were built into wipes so I wouldn't have to be intentional about finding a bottle of cleaner and a rag. Yes these items are less cost effective, but I ask you this: how much are your weekends worth? I buy bulk and stock each bathroom and the kitchen with their own multipurpose wipes and window/mirror wipes. Every couple of days when I notice a buildup of spots or tooth paste spills, all I have to do is reach under the sink and grab a wipe.

Maybe you're reading this and thinking, *I can't find someone for $65 in my town*, or, *I've already made every cut I can and $65 more is not possible*. Sister, pray! The God of this universe loves you so much and cares about you enough that He hears your heart. If this is your struggle, needing your weekends back and freedom in your time and space, then pray. God can send you a Helen like he sent me, or maybe he's got a creative answer for you. Perhaps you watch your friends' kids for a few hours in exchange for her cleaning for you. You do not need to be wealthy or living with excess to figure this one out. There are websites and apps like Nextdoor and Care.com where you can post a specific advertisement and limit the audience so you don't get a bunch of serial killers showing up in your home. On Nextdoor, I've seen many advertisements posted seeking childcare, cleaning, or pet sitting in exchange for other services. If you connect with someone who has a need, maybe you can meet it and get your house cleaned in the meantime! Who knows, you might even make a new friend. This also may be an opportunity to tap into your stay-at-home mom friends. I have a few I am certain would come clean my house for two hours in exchange for my taking their kids to the park or pool for them. Sometimes the little escape, even if it is to your friend's house to scrub floors, is worth the tradeoff.

Laundry is another task that plagued our weekends for far too many years. I finally found a solution that worked for our family that I share on my blog at fortheworkingmama.com with a link to the hamper that makes it all possible. My oldest currently wears uniforms, and with my old laundry routine I would have needed twenty-two of them to keep her fully dressed for more than a week. New laundry me, however, can rotate six uniforms with such ease. The best part is, there is never laundry anywhere but where it belongs. If you do the weekly dump on your dining room table, I think you are allowing yourself to be prisoner to the laundry. Don't even take it out of the kids' rooms until you are ready to do something about it. And resist the urge to do that quick changeover to mass-produce clean clothes if the day doesn't allow for you to fold them and put them away. Break free of the chains of laundry! It is much better off housed in the places it belongs, even if you have to hide your bikini under that dress.

I resist the urge to write out all of the household chores in a weekly calendar and assign various tasks to each weekday. This may work for you, but for me it creates opportunity for failure. Each day holds some unexpected challenge or blessing that can derail a very regimented chore schedule and leave you feeling like your to-do list is mounting. I keep plenty of room in the margins of my list for things to come up because I want to be interrupted. I want to be able to bring a meal to someone in need or stop by a friend's house for coffee if invited. I want to be able to pull out the Play-Doh and paint set to get creative with my kids, even if the counters aren't wiped down or I didn't get to that day's laundry basket. This is where you let go of your idea of perfection and welcome some spontaneous disruptions. Your unfinished task will be waiting that evening or the next day, unless you've got some magical elves that come in and make it all disappear.

- **Streamline your morning routine.** The art of getting yourself and your kids out the door in the morning can seem as difficult as an Iron Man race in the middle of the Sahara. I don't have the luxury of entering the car line with my pajamas on and a cup of coffee in hand. As a working mama, I'm sure you can relate. We have to be dressed for the job long before we are required to arrive.

In the past, I would wake up later than I wanted, rush to finish a million things, and then try to find thirty to forty minutes to do my hair. Just my hair! And I don't even live in Texas. There are far too many mornings to count when I would finally strap in to the driver's seat with my blood pressure off the charts. By that point,

I'd yelled at at least one human and two dogs, and sometimes tears were involved, often my own.

This is no way to start your day. It sounds dramatic, but it's for real. So, I found a new way to do this. I showered at night; invested in some top-notch Drybar dry shampoo to look fresh in the morning; shrank my morning to-do list to dress, eat, coffee, and devotion; and took all the other pressure off to do anything else. My kids eat dry cereal in a Ziploc baggie or toaster waffle on the drive to school, we pray for their day in the carline, and off they go. They don't miss the hot breakfast buffet they never had. I will not feel guilty for that, and neither should you!

On occasion I sacrifice that quick devotion, and it's amazing how that tiny tilt in my daily axis can send me into a whole new orbit. Not to mention the morning sets the tone for everything that follows. When I curse and cry before I even hit the interstate, imagine how well my body and mind react to the stress of the morning commute. It is just a recipe for the ultimate bad day. I've often left the kids at drop off and been hit by the wave of guilt that starts the second round of tears before I can even pull out of the parking lot. If a morning like this is so destructive for my own wellbeing, how am I setting my kids up for a successful day? Making tiny changes to the morning like laying out their clothes, socks, shoes, and hairpieces the night before, packing their lunches and backpacks up in the evening, and bathing them at night minimizes their morning responsibilities as well. I often will even load up every item that doesn't have to be refrigerated into the car in the evening, including the baggie of dry cereal, so that we can literally dress and hop in. If I could guarantee we would wake up looking fresh, we would sleep in our clothes. When we enter the car, we listen to music that is uplifting and encouraging, and I am daily doing my best to let my kids see *this* version of their mom. It's good for them, and it's even better for me, because that is a soul that radiates the Spirit within me.

- **Clear your mind and organize your headspace.** As working moms we have an extra special confusion when it comes to keeping our calendar organized because we juggle more than one. For years I tried to make the iPhone calendar system exclusively work for me. The phone calendar linked with my work Outlook calendar, so I felt like this would keep all the things in one place. I was not aware that others in my organization had access to see things that were on my calendar, and when someone asked me if I was off for the week because my calendar was blocked and said, "No school. Find Ella childcare," I about spit my coffee out. I was going back through all of the many personal things I had tagged on my own calendar, including "Schedule GYN appointment to get IUD changed," and wondering who I had been enlightening on all the inner workings of my personal schedule and reproductive system. After a series of issues with balancing everything on this tiny device I carried in my purse, I decided I am just a person who likes paper. I need a visual of the day, the week, the month and a place to make myself notes to get the clutter out of my head, to schedule GYN appointments and kid pickups without all the world seeing them.

So I broke every rule of my millennial generation's dependency on technology and invested in an old-school paper planner. I cycled through several brands, styles, and variations until I found the one that met all of my needs and was high enough quality to withstand going with me literally everywhere I go. If you are going to carry this thing with you on the regular, you probably also want it to be cute. So I landed on the Simplified Planner. Yes, it's expensive ($58 for the daily, plus shipping), but I'm so confident its quality and layout will meet all of my needs that I am going on my third edition. I started out with the weekly edition and found I didn't have enough space to empty all the clutter in my head and was still having to carry around a notebook with it. I made the switch to the daily edition, and let's just say, game changer! There is enough space on each page to write out your daily appointments as well as take notes in all your meetings. I can make my work and home to-do lists on the same page, and I use this as a place to upload what is in my brain and free up mental capacity. If I have thoughts of something I need to remember or an idea I don't want to execute now but don't want to forget, I jot it there and allow my mind to release it.

We carry so many thoughts in our head, constantly juggling any number of things. Find a way that works for you to free up some space in your mind. Just like our computers or phones that have limited space and need backing up to a cloud to make room for more, define a system for your own life that is your mental cloud. My planner is so much more than a calendar. While I love it for the schedule organization and the space it gives me to write all of my daily personal and work commitments, it is a journal of sorts. I take all my meeting notes on the page for the day the meeting took place. My company still uses Outlook invites and a virtual calendar that I populate with work meetings and the like, but everything gets written in my planner so I have a physical backup in the event of those technological meltdowns and a place to combine the personal and professional obligations.

- **Stop the phone from interrupting your evening.** If you need more time in your day to keep your home organized and tidy and do all the other mom things, I'm going to hand you the gift of time right here. I will provide caution that this may be more humiliating than standing in front of a full-length mirror naked, but you have to know where you started to realize the magnitude of where you end up. If you have an iPhone, grab that baby right now and go into Settings. Find where it says, "Screen time," and prepare for total shock. I've been intentionally good about my phone lately and am still averaging three hours a day. That is a lot of time to be staring down at a tiny screen. Once you've identified how much time you have up for grabs, implement a couple of systems to help you cut back on screen time in the after-work hours.

  The first is setting up VIP contacts. Despite all of my best efforts, I could not embrace abandoning my email after hours because there were a handful of people in my organization who would send time-sensitive things. So instead of grabbing my phone every time it buzzed or chimed to indicate an incoming email, I set those few people as VIP contacts and gave them a separate ringtone. When the phone buzzed thirty times an evening with nonsense I wasn't a prisoner to it. If I heard the specific VIP chime,

I knew it was something I should glance at, which is simple because only your VIP emails preview on your lock screen.

The second phone tip you can implement is choosing a two-hour block when you get home to put your phone on "Do Not Disturb" with an auto-text reply. You could have it read something like, "I'm sorry I'm not seeing your text right now. From the hours of 6 P.M. to 8 P.M. we are having family time. I will respond as soon as we get the kids to bed." That's it! Then you are off the hook from responding to anyone during those precious two hours in the evening with your kids. It's also teaching those who text you that you are not afraid to value what is important. We get less done in the evening when we have so many distractions, so eliminate some of them by putting the phone down!

- And, drumroll please for the last tip that will change your life: **Grocery delivery service.** Bam! There it is, the Holy Grail, the golden cup. You maybe read that and immediately dismissed it, saying it's only for the rich. Well, ladies, I used to waste so much money taking my kids to the grocery store. In order to just make it through with minimal drama, we'd end up with opened cereal and Cheez-Its, half-eaten granola bars, juice boxes with the character heads, and randomness like expandable sponges or light-up finger light sabers. (Seriously, Publix, why?)

Grocery delivery rolled out in our little town about eight months ago. It was $14 a month plus tip, with a 7% markup on groceries. I thought this all sounded like a waste of money for something I was capable of doing, but it was new and shiny, and I wanted to give it a try to see if it had life-changing potential. After three months, I was hooked. Sure, I'm spending a little extra on tip and the percentage increase, but my grocery bill is $60–$90 less per week. A typical Alexander house trip to the grocery store lands me about $175–$230 a week for our usual staples, evening meals, and all the cash wrap items my kids must have or they might die. On Shipt, our grocery delivery service, I spend $110–$165, including the tip and service fee. It lets you re-buy your usual items with ease and still see what's on sale. It is the ultimate in anti-impulse buying and gives me back the 2–3 hours of frustration going up and down every aisle with a toddler or wasting my Saturday in the aisle of Publix. When I know another mama who is a little too stretched on time and needs some simplicity, I gift Shipt for her birthday. This is also the ultimate in new mom gifts and makes a great baby shower present. Everyone fights it because it feels like a wasteful indulgence, but once they are forced to give it a try because it's gifted, it unlocks the miracle of this service.

If your town doesn't have this service yet, I pray for you it comes soon. Maybe you have a grocery pickup option, which can save time and have the same reduction in frivolous spending. We still go to the grocery store once every couple of months to make a last-minute pickup or shop for a party, and each time we are reminded just how blessed we are by this service!

The number one question people ask me when they find out I'm a working mom is, "How do you have time for all of this stuff?" By stuff, they mean keeping my house clean, letting my kids be in activities, serving at my church, leading a Bible study, and writing a book. I think they ask because they see I work full-time and on the surface things seem to be relatively "together." They also ask because I don't walk around saying I'm tired, stressed, or overwhelmed. I am ALL of those things on the regular, but to dwell on them only makes the mountain seem bigger. I find time, I find solutions, I draw ideas from other people who have survived these particular battles before me, and I have no problem copying their methods. Simplifying tasks, letting certain things go, and, on occasion, paying people to do things for me (even if money is tight) creates time where time does not exist. It lets me build in extra playtime, time alone with my husband, or time for myself for some soul-care.

Finding fixes for the mom issues that cause you the most stress will allow you to achieve your new standard of perfection, your very own "good enough." Streamlining your chores and freeing up your weekend will deliver the added benefit of de-cluttering your mind to find rest for your soul. This is a lesson I learned from my mama!

Chapter 3

It Takes a Village: We Were Not Meant for Isolation

The end of the world is coming soon. Therefore be earnest and disciplined in your prayers. Most important of all continue to show deep love for each other, for love covers a multitude of sins. Cheerfully share your home with those who need a meal or a place to stay. God has given each of you a gift from His great variety of spiritual gifts. Use them well to serve one another.
1 Peter 4:7–10

In my late teens, a horror movie came out about a village. The people were confined to this village surrounded by woods and terrified about what lived beyond. In addition to being frightened by the creatures that lived in the woods, I was fascinated with this village. Simplicity, community, and creativity abounded inside its boundaries. The people had deeper friendships because of their isolation, protected one another, and learned to use the greatest resource they had in this village—each other. This idea of community resonates so deeply because I believe that you and I were created with an innate desire for relational living. There have been seasons in my life when being active in my village has come easier than other times, but I never needed this more than as a working mom.

When you pare down what you have and whom you have around

you like the characters in the village of the movie, you learn to allow people into your real life, the messy parts. When there are fewer distractions cluttering your daily planner, you can take time to stop and open the door and let people in. This concept of needing people to do life with is not reserved for Hollywood films. You and I—we need people. And not just any people. We need real friends. We were not designed to go at it alone. After all, in the very first scene of humanity, when God created us, He looked at Adam and said, "It is not good for the man to be alone" (Genesis 2:18). Isolation is where the enemy wants us. We are no threat to the advancing of the gospel when we stay locked in our houses behind piles of chores or at our desks with our heads down focused on the task at hand. If we can predict and count on just one thing to be true of our futures, it is the fact that we are not exempt from hardship, sorrow, loss, or disappointment. This life will have difficulties, and when those times come, being able to rely on a person or small group of people is what will carry you through.

Whoever said, "It takes a village" deserves a cookie. I can accomplish very little in my home and professional lives without, at the very minimum, the prayerful support of my village. If you picked up this book on a mission to fill a void and find a deeper purpose for your own life, finding people to do this with is arguably the most important step. In Ecclesiastes we hear from a rich man, Solomon, as he tells us that life is about more than just riches: "Two people are better off than one, for they can help each other succeed" (Ecclesiastes 4:19).

I could find a million reasons why I don't have time for this type of community outside the four walls of my home because I have a job, a husband, and all kinds of mom responsibilities. What I've come to learn and embrace through the ups and downs of my life struggles is that I can't afford *not* to surround myself with people. There are times when someone from my village will make a deposit into my soul when I haven't an ounce of my own strength left. We all need a group of people who support and encourage us, people whom we call when we find ourselves in need of a lifeline.

A village is not just your friends or your family; it's a ring (or rings) of people who invest in your life and whose lives you reciprocate into.

Our calling in this short life is to make an impact by drawing others to Jesus, and the most powerful way to do that is by being relational. Maybe you're reading this and still not tracking with me. Or maybe you don't have your village yet. Let me tell you a little bit about mine and then encourage you to find yours.

I think of my village as a bull's-eye, with a core and outer rings. All levels of that bull's-eye are equally valuable, but they serve different purposes. My husband, Chris, is my best friend. He has been since we were fifteen years old. I found the love of my life in first period geography class in tenth grade, and he became my person. I had girl friends throughout high school and college, but as you move through stages of life, some people don't move with you. This was true of those girl friends. At twenty years old, Chris and I walked down a flower-lined aisle with so much tulle to Nick Lachey's song "This I Swear." We stepped into the church that day as two independent young adults and stepped out as a family.

With all this change transitioning into adulthood, I knew we couldn't do life alone. We needed new, grown-up friends, people at different ages and stages of their lives who could give us wisdom and instruction. It was as if there was a yearning inside of me for connection with women and desperation for a support system. We lived an hour from my family, which might as well have been a whole hemisphere away because you don't do daily life together when there's an hour drive between you. More than friends, I needed a Tampa family. I needed people to love on me, support me, and build me up in my new career, my marriage, and my quest for motherhood. These people could only be found in one place: God's house. I signed up for a women's life group that met one day a week, not knowing anyone ahead of time. My desire to belong to a group was far stronger than any insecurity I had about fitting in, so when the leader called me before it started to introduce herself and seemed nice enough, I decided to show up. That one decision to step out in awkward faith and put myself out there as the new girl has shaped so many aspects of my life.

I met the first ring of my village in that life group—the core of my bull's-eye. Together we are an unlikely bunch of sisters who now range from thirty-five to seventy years old, from married with kids to divorced, from working to staying at home to retired, from outgoing to introverted. We are all God-fearing, Jesus-loving women who have been pulling up dining room chairs for over a decade to do life together. These women prayed for me over my battle with infertility, brought me coffee and flowers and coffee cake in the hospital when I had my babies, cried with me when I miscarried, and squealed in excitement when I had positive pregnancy tests. They hold my hand when my mom is too far away, cook me meals when I'm down and out, and would drop anything in an instant to be at my doorstep with just a single call. I know this because they have done it all. In my darkest of days, when loss and anxiety and depression were words I was all too familiar with, they would not let me walk alone.

The honest truth is that life with a new baby is hard. There are so many joys and excitements that come with that little baby, but I was not prepared for all the pressures of parenting, the hormonal changes, and the strain it would place on our marriage. We were two very selfish people who did not want to give up our independence. We also struggled with the shift in our attention. I was obsessed with my baby—if you saw her baby pictures you'd understand why! —And I pushed pause on being a wife and just wanted to own this motherhood thing. I didn't seek out time with Chris, I didn't meet his needs, and in return he neglected mine. I can confidently admit that so much of this was escalated as a result of my battle with postpartum depression. It didn't present itself in the way the stereotypes describe because it wasn't an endless sadness that made me not want to bond with my baby. It was masked in a deep and uncontrollable anxiety.

I knew the Lord, I knew the peace and joy that can come from Him, and so I struggled with the battle between faith and mental health. I wondered, was I just weak in faith or did I need medical intervention? Truth be told, I was too prideful to face this issue as a medical one. It was the darkest place I had ever been mentally, and it was embarrassing and humiliating. But it was too much a burden to carry alone. I needed to take it somewhere, and there was only one place I felt comfortable doing so—the core, the first ring of my village. These women are my "Bible study Babes". I hadn't yet exposed them to any of these parts of who I was capable of becoming, so I was fearful that they would change their opinion of me or reject me completely when I decided to get real with them, but I knew I could no longer go at this battle alone.

They were relentless in their love, grace, and accountability. In fact, it bordered on annoying when all I wanted to do was crawl into a cave. When I finally opened up about my struggles and exposed my weaknesses and shortcomings to them, the support, encouragement, and reassurances overwhelmed me. It was as if Jesus had stepped down off the heavenly throne and wrapped His loving arms around me in the form of these women.

With their support, I sought medical help and went on an antidepressant to help control the lows. Slowly, with that assistance and my faith, I started to get back to myself. I could have never done it alone, and I was too embarrassed to go to my family. I couldn't walk through it with Chris either because he was too close to the situation. I needed these women, this group. We are a perfectly imperfect mess where you can come as you are and always be accepted.

Maybe you're hearing this and envying my village. Maybe you always wanted to belong to something like this but never found the opportunity. Well, sister, let me just tell you, this took work. It took five women, dedicated to Jesus first and each other second, who wouldn't give up. There were times when our group grew to ten or twelve, but the five Babes have been around since the beginning. We have gone through seasons when the enemy has played tricks on our minds, telling us that isolation is better than our circle, that our sins are too great to be accepted by this group, that our pain is too deep to share, that our faults and struggles are too embarrassing for us to face each other. But someone (and this role is constantly evolving) always steps up to the plate and offers exactly the reassurance that the hurting one needs. She points back to the truth, she comforts, and she embraces.

There is no perfect person or designated leader in our group. We all take turns being in the hot seat (it's literally the chair to the right of the head of the table), and we all take turns stepping in to comfort and walk through someone else's struggle. If you don't have something like this, if you don't have a place where you can pull up a chair and always be welcomed, seek prayer and support, or phone a friend when you need it most. Go out and get it. Sign up for a Bible study, small group, MOPS, or whatever it takes to find like-minded women. If the first group doesn't click, try another. Pray that God gives you this foundation in your life, and that He raises up women who can be your village, who can hold you accountable and keep you on the path He has for your life. Trust me, you need this more than you know! If you're thinking right now, *Yeah right. When do I have time for this?* Then start one in your own house at a time that works for you. Or, at the very least, join an online community. This is 2019; the possibilities are endless!

My Babes are the core of my village, and then the next ring is our couples' Bible study group that our church calls "life group." We have made the investment in our marriage to be in a couples' life group since early on. When I first proposed the idea to Chris, two years after we were married, he was hesitant but eventually agreed to try one. After our first semester with a group, he said he felt like the content wasn't rich enough, the connection wasn't deep enough, and the friendships were not growing strong enough. On our ride home from group one night, I challenged him to step out and lead one in our home if he didn't feel he was finding what he was looking for in our existing group. Like most of the challenges he faces in his life, Chris accepted and took it on full force, and as a result we have had the most incredible run of couples' life groups in our home. They build the same type of love and accountability as in my women's group but for us as a couple. Our first group in our home grew into a tight-knit family. They laid hands on me before our first fertility procedure, celebrated and showered us for our first pregnancy, and brought us food (it's always food with church people!) when they saw the dark circles under our eyes from sleepless nights and wanted to take some of the burden. We walked through the highs and low of our life together and rallied in both excitement and loss.

Regardless of transitions and change, we have prioritized this for more than a decade. Today, we host a diverse and beautiful group of people on Monday nights when our kids are sleeping. When we started this group we encountered the same fears: What if no one shows up? What if no one connects? And more importantly, what if they are all weirdoes? And just like all the times before, God did not disappoint in

His delivery of an incredible group. Today, we have sixteen people from different walks of life who share what is on their hearts and celebrate in answered prayers that could fill all the pages of this book. We tell stories and laugh, and on occasion someone cries. Where two or more are gathered, God promises to be there also, and each Monday night He shows up at our home on Tideline Drive.

We are not always eager for the first doorbell to ring. In fact, most Mondays feel like we've been through the Ninja Warrior obstacle course fifty times just to get us to 7:30 P.M. Our kids are a little more difficult to get to bed than other nights, our house needs a quick cleanup, sometimes I burn the Toll House chocolate chip cookies or the coffee pot overflows and spills all over the floor. On occasion I'm so tired I can't fathom having to muster a complete sentence let alone small talk followed by questions. But in a miracle as great as turning water into wine, Jesus turns our souls the minute the first couple walks through our door. We have supernatural energy and enthusiasm and love for each other, and the evening flies by with incredible ease. At 10:00 P.M., when Chris and I are moving our dining room chairs back to the table and cleaning up the coffee mess, we often look at each other and say, "I'm so glad we met." We started as perfect strangers and became family through Christ. It's the most wonderful transformation made beautiful by the hand of God. It is men and women saying to each other, to their kids they leave at home, to their jobs, and to the world, "I put this at the top of my list."

If you've tried to get your man to join a group and he's greeted you with resistance, that's normal. 90% of the men in our group said they would never have joined had their wives not pushed it. The beauty is, those very same men now show up alone on weeks when their wives can't make it. Don't nag them, ladies; it will never work. Ask humbly and pray. It's all you can do. If your relationship is strained and you're thinking, *This is just what we need*, nagging your husband into it would be as effective as knocking him upside the head with a frying pan. Pray that God works on his heart, pray that God plants the desire and that He will bring one other person into your husband's life to invite him or encourage him to attend a group so that the pressure is not all on you. Even after Chris agreed to go, it took a few weeks of prayer and another man at our church reaching out to invite him to get the actual commitment. Men are different than us! If you say, "Let's go to a shooting range or a golf course," they are all in because they don't have to talk. But if you say, let's go sit in a room of perfect strangers and divulge our most intimate feelings in long, drawn-out conversations, they would probably rather be water boarded. If they've never been to a group, then they don't know what to expect and don't know the amazing benefit of belonging. So pray, on your knees, right now and know I'm praying with you.

While our churches have been amazing sources for our village over the years, we are not Christians who live in a bubble. There are so many other people we encounter outside of our church circle who make up the third ring of our village. Our church friends feed our soul, hold us spiritually accountable, and provide such prayerful support. Our third ring provides the practical and hands-on support to make it through each day. These are the neighbors and friends who make up the emergency contact list at my kids' schools. They are the people who know when Chris is out of town and I need an extra hand. I could not get through a crazy week of work and family life without these people. God has strategically placed them in my life, and they are an unlikely bunch. They don't collaborate in their efforts to be my village, but I would classify them all in this same ring. This third ring is my neighbors, my babysitters, and my cousin Brandon.

One of these third-ring villagers is my neighbor Colleen. In August of 2013, when I was just entering my thirties, I met the most selfless mama I will ever know in Colleen. We had moved from our home of ten years to a new town about forty-five minutes away. I felt alienated from the life we'd lived before but excited about what this new opportunity would hold. We moved into our house with the lot to our right empty, and I would constantly run to the dining room window any time I heard movement to see what house would pop up and who would occupy it. When that house was finished, I watched the move-in take place from that same window with such anticipation. As the last of the boxes were unloaded, I decided it was time to do the neighborly (nosy) thing and walk over with some cookies.

When Colleen answered the door, she was so warm and welcoming and bent down to greet Ella face-to-face. She expressed her excitement to be on our street and apologized for not making it over to meet us yet. We stood in her doorway and talked for a few minutes about our jobs and our families. After exchanging basic introductions, she somewhat reluctantly asked if I would like to meet her little girl. Before I could answer, Ella yelled, "YES!" She was so excited to have a little friend next door, and to be honest, the only reason she agreed to join me on this cookie delivery was hopeful anticipation of a new bestie. A few seconds later, Colleen came back around the corner with the most precious little face I had ever seen. Her beautiful little girl was nestled into her shoulder and curved into her mama's body as if she were designed to fit there. I could see that Quinn was an extraordinary little girl. This little angel next door was born with a rare brain disorder. While her life looked so much different than my girls', it had an incredible impact on countless people. Quinn would never walk or talk, she would never skip or run or skin her knees from falling, but she would light up a room with a smile that went from ear to ear and eyes that had an extra special little sparkle.

As our friendship progressed, I had the privilege of watching Colleen love this little girl so big that I could see exactly why God had entrusted this precious one to her. I gained an incredible perspective watching their love and Colleen's sacrifices to give Quinn everything in life possible. We shared many memories with Quinn in her short little life, and her mama is one who deserves a medal! This woman went to work and came home each day to serve her home with such balance. In all of our years of friendship, I have never once heard her utter a complaint about her situation or a comparison to others who weren't dealt her hand.

The day of Quinn's funeral, when we celebrated her little life and her journey into heaven, was one of those days I will forever remember. From the same dining room window in my house where I had waited in anticipation with the curtains peeled back for a house to be built, waited as a moving truck filled it with the belongings of our new neighbors, I now watched Colleen walk to her car for the most difficult day of her life. She was dressed in a stunning black dress, and her hair was smooth and styled. Her gaze was down at her feet, and she appeared to be focusing on the act of putting one foot in front of the other. A few minutes later we joined her and her family and an enormous number of supporters at Saint Anne Catholic Church to pay tribute to Quinn's life. Her mama had to do the unbearable; she had to say goodbye to her sweet little baby for her remaining time on earth and trust that one day she would see her again. Just writing those words brings me back to that day and the unexplainable sorrow of watching a mother and father walk a tiny little casket draped in pink roses down an aisle filled with tear-stained faces. In my human mind, I want to ask the whys, like why do things like this have to be a part of our story? Why should any mama have to burry her child? We won't have answers to these questions until we meet the Lord face-to-face, but we can have comfort in His promises.

I watched Colleen grieve her little girl in a way that demonstrated more faith than I had ever seen displayed in the life of another. Her life will never be the same, and there will always be a hole in her heart, but she continues to live. She knows life is precious. As I watched her walk through this difficult season, I did the only thing I knew to do: I tried to show up, to be *her* village. I didn't always have words to say or ways to comfort, but God showed me I just needed to be there. In those moments of running out for bagels in the morning with no makeup and red eyes that revealed evidence of a night of crying or taking a walk through our neighborhood late at night just to blow off steam, what God was doing was so immeasurable. I wasn't called to show up to be there for Colleen; she was showing up to be there for me. She was teaching me what it really means to walk by faith and demonstrating what a real dependency on the Lord looks like. Colleen taught me selfless love and wild faith.

A true village is not just about people pouring into your life; it's an opportunity for you to serve others. When we talk about awakening our souls for a life more fulfilling, I can think of no greater evidence of this than the opportunities I have had to be someone else's village.

When I asked Colleen if I could share part of her story, she reminded me that her greatest goal in life is to use the story God wrote for her life to encourage others. She wanted it written down *for you* because maybe your little one has gone to be with the Lord or you struggle daily to meet the needs of your child who doesn't get to be "normal" by the world's standards. Or perhaps, just like me, you need a little perspective. Hopefully the story of this selfless mama can be a beautiful picture of the love God has for us, of His laying down His Son's life so we may have ours. It is also a constant reminder that when we don't embrace our village and invite people into the messy parts of life, we are missing out on so many blessings that God has for this life. Back to Solomon's thoughts on having people to do life with, he warns, "If one person falls, the other can reach out and help. But someone who falls alone is in real trouble" (Ecclesiastes 4:10).

In the same way that God allowed me to be present for Colleen during her fall, He used the life of another to walk alongside me through my own. The story I am about to tell you is to help you, the working mama, realize why it is so important to create this sense of community in your workplace—the fourth ring of the bull's-eye. Life does not reserve the trials and complications for nights and weekends. A battle can come up from any angle at any time of the day, and chances are, you will go through some stuff between the hours of nine and five. In June of 2013, I experienced the hardest emotional fall of my life, my greatest loss and sorrow, and it happened while I was at work. I did not have to do this alone because I had allowed people into my life, into my village, even when it wasn't convenient, easy, or something I had time for.

I was not always focused on building community in my workplace. It wasn't until I met Jamie that I learned to look up. Jamie always greeted everyone with a smile. She talked to strangers, she stopped to help those who looked lost, and she allowed her life to be a series of interruptions to meet the needs of those she encountered. My work village began with just Jamie and today has grown to include many. But it's that one, the very first real and deep connection I made at work, which has woven its way into this story.

When Ella was three years old, we decided it was time to add to our family. We revisited the same fertility specialists we had seen prior, and after almost an entire year of drugs and two failed procedures, we pushed pause on the aggressive treatments and decided that maybe God had already given us what we were supposed to have. Then, in a routine visit with my gynecologist, she encouraged me to participate in an off-label use drug trial for fertility. One of the causes linked to polycystic ovarian syndrome is an insulin issue. My gynecologist had just read a journal article on the use of metformin, a drug commonly used to treat diabetes, to treat infertility in PCOS patients. The side effects were far less severe than the long list of possibilities from the fertility drugs, and for fifteen dollars I figured it was worth a try. The metformin came in a six-month dose, and after I took that last pill, I dismissed the idea that this was going to result in a pregnancy and continued on with life. I had closed the door on expanding our family and resolved that Ella was our one and only miracle baby.

We were moving out of our first home, busy packing and de-cluttering ten years of hoarding, when I came across a pregnancy test in my bathroom. I started to process when my last cycle was, if there was any possibility that I was pregnant. I decided there was nothing to lose and it had probably expired anyway, so I took it. I nervously laughed and carried the stick to Chris, who was packing our kitchen, and I uttered the words, "I think I'm pregnant." He stood there wide-eyed with our dinner plates in hand and barely said a word for a full minute. After months of trying and two failed treatments, this just seemed so impossible to believe. We were ecstatic and overjoyed, but I'd be lying to say we both completely believed it in that moment. A call to my OB and a couple of blood tests confirmed the news.

The pregnancy was progressing until I found myself in the ER at ten weeks on a Sunday evening. What had started as light spotting earlier in the week had become to enough bleeding to cause concern. The ultrasound technician on the weekend night shift in the ER did an ultrasound, and I got my first view of that little baby I already loved. They said things were fine and sent me home. The following Monday I went to see my doctor during my lunch break for what should have been a fairly routine visit. I went alone because we had just been told everything was okay the day before. It only took her a few short minutes to utter the words I will never forget. It was abrupt, scientific, and matter-of-fact, without any emotion. "Miscarriage." I burst into tears. I sat there in the sterile room, a sobbing and stunned mess.

The doctor said that if I could bear a bit of discomfort she would be able to perform a quick procedure in the office that would prevent me from needing any follow-up care. The thought of physical discomfort could not have compared to the pain I felt emotionally, so I obliged. Within a matter of minutes she had extracted what she referred to as "tissue," but to me, it was my baby. She wrapped it in paper dressings and disposed of it in that special red trashcan filled with bio hazardous waste. She patted my knee, said, "Everything will be okay," and exited the room. I sat on that exam table in utter shock. I was hysterical, sobbing. I could barely catch my breath. I wanted to jump off the table, open that trashcan, and sort through it until I found the paper containing my baby, but I could not get off the table. I reached for my cell phone, and I called on someone from my village at work, someone I knew would be there in no time, someone I was confident would just hold me.

Jamie arrived and did exactly that. She helped me finish getting dressed and stand to my feet. She cried with me, walked me to my car, told me she loved me, and did not tell me that it would all be okay. I didn't want to hear that. I wanted to understand how a loving God could give me this gift out of the blue just to take it away. I needed to know how you tell four-year-old who was so excited to be a big sister that her dreams are no longer. How do you make yourself whole again when something that was growing in your body is taken out and discarded in a trashcan? It was a pain I had never experienced in the deepest part of my core. I had already walked through the battle of anxiety and depression, but this was so much different.

As I drove home from that appointment, I cried out to God. It was audible, loud, and angry. I said, "Why, God? Why would you do this? Why did you even allow me to be pregnant just to take it away?" I banged on the steering wheel, I screamed, and I sobbed. I had to deliver the news to my husband on the phone, and hearing him well up in tears just ripped open the wound deeper.

In all of God's love and grace, He used the tiniest of humans to begin to heal our hearts—our Ella. All of His wisdom and a deep understanding came flowing out of a four-year-old little girl. She comforted Chris, she soothed me, and she spoke words that prove children have such innocent faith and a special connection with God. As she stroked our backs, she said, "Mommy and Daddy, it's okay that we lost this baby. It was a boy, but God told me we will have a girl." If those words don't give you goose bumps, let me finish the story!

I went for a follow-up with my GYN two days later, and she gave me controversial advice yet again. This same doctor who had encouraged me into the off-label use of metformin that resulted in the pregnancy and miscarriage told me to try again, now. She said, "There is very little evidence that links one miscarriage to potential for others. Most women miscarry at least once in their lives without ever knowing it. Your best chances of being fertile are immediately following. I'd like you to try to get pregnant right away if you're up for it." I've talked to many women since who have received very conflicting advice from their physicians, so I would advise you to always consult your own doctor because they know your situation best. However, for me, this advice would shape what comes next. I filed this directive in the back of my mind, and we didn't do anything to prevent it. Exactly one month later, on July 17, 2013, I was walking by the pharmacy near work and felt compelled to buy a test. I took it in the hallway bathroom at my office, and there it was, in blue, a big fat plus sign.

God had a plan. He wanted me to walk through this trial to show me how big He could be, to show me the meaning of childlike faith, and to allow me to challenge Him and see that He would still love me. He wanted me to rely on others in my brokenness and cling to Him in the valley of the shadow of death. On March 23, 2014, we welcomed a little miracle baby *girl*, Meadow India Alexander. It was a girl! Ella, at four years old, was exactly right, because God had told her. I believe to my core that when I get to heaven one day I will have a little boy I never got to meet coming to say hello. But until then, our earthly family is complete with these two sweet, independent, strong, and confident little girls.

Your family is your family. They will always love you, but they have to! The amazing thing about finding your village is allowing people to love you because they choose to and doing the same for them in return. It's an opportunity to make a meaningful impact in the lives of others and feel it right back. My village does not just do for me; I also delight in opportunities to meet their needs, pray alongside them, and lift them up with encouragement.

As a working mama, your time is likely limited. I don't have hours to spend going out for happy hour or ladies' night, but it takes me only a few intentional minutes to send a word of encouragement to someone struggling, drop a meal off for someone who is sick or has had a baby, order a book for someone I know needs the wisdom, or call someone who is hurting on my commute home and just let them talk. When I select a handful of people to connect with in a deep way, the fruits, the results, are so sweet. The depth of the relationships grows beyond the superficial so you can feel this connection to your friends in Christ.

Your village doesn't have to be large. It can be a small circle of people, even two or three. One is a great place to start. Build your core and work your way out so you too can eat well! Once you've built it, don't be afraid to ask for help from your people. This is my biggest fault because whether it's my pride or not wanting to inconvenience people, I will try something 150 ways before I ask someone to help me. That is, until I'm faced with a situation like that day in the doctor's office with the miscarriage, when I knew it was impossible to stand on my own two feet by my own strength. I will forever remember the look on Jamie's face when she opened the door and met me in the exam room, her eyes red and already filled with tears. I was unable to contain the sobs, and my shoulders were shaking with each inhale. Jamie knew I would be too embarrassed to walk past the waiting room full of expectant moms there for routine checkups, so she hugged me close and shielded my face so we could quickly make our way to the elevator. She was broken for me, and her face told me that I had permission to feel this excruciating sadness and disappointment. I'm confident God did something that changed our friendship forever that day. She knew after that she was the one person I could let see me like that, and I knew she was the one who would show up. On March 23, 2014, Jamie showed up again in my delivery room to encourage me through labor and then again to meet Meadow after she entered the world.

More than just finding your village, ladies, call on them when you need them. God created us for this type of community, and fortunately for us, we are not living in that horror film I referenced at the beginning of this chapter in order to find it. I guarantee that if you take an inventory of the people in your life today you can begin to piece this together enough to understand where the gaps are. This may take work, and you may have to be intentional in order to find it, but one thing is certain: you were not created to live this life on your own.

Chapter 3 Application
Define your village

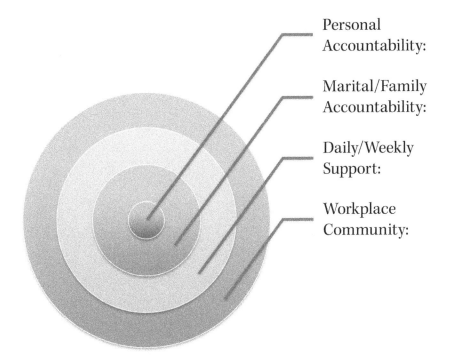

Personal Accountability:

Marital/Family Accountability:

Daily/Weekly Support:

Workplace Community:

A soul set on fire for a more fulfilled life often requires someone else to spark the flame when you've let it go out. This isn't just about who's helping to light your fire but how can you be the ignition in the lives of others. You cannot do this life alone; it goes against who God designed us to be. Make a commitment to yourself to find your village or embrace it today. Fill in the names of the people who represent your village. Where you have visual gaps, pray over those areas that God would bring the people in your circle right there where you need them.

If you are not part of a body of believers who share your faith and encourage you in the spiritual battles, I encourage you to build it. On www.fortheworkingmama.com, in the Chapter 3 application section, you will find everything you need to start a life group. Don't be intimidated; just follow the steps listed out and let God do the rest.

Chapter 4

The Other Camp: Us vs. Them

Finally, all of you should be of one mind. Sympathize
with each other. Love each other as brothers and sisters.
Be tenderhearted, and keep a humble attitude.
1 Peter 3:8

Warning: This chapter may not be suitable for stay-at-home mamas. If that is you, I'm so thankful you decided to give this book a read. But I kindly suggest you skip this one. It's not for you, I promise. In fact, it's a place for me as a working mom to get real with the judgment and insecurities that come from friendships with lovely women like you. Some of it is rooted in jealousy, whether or not we working mamas want to admit it, because from our vantage point it looks like your life is easier with far less stress. When we hear you complain about a long day or a lack of help from your spouse, there is a tiny piece of us that may or may not want to punch you in the face (not literally, of course, but with words . . . definitely with words). And it's not because we don't like you; it's because we don't speak the same code. When my feet hit the floor in the morning, my day looks quite a bit different than yours. It begins with the mad dash to get out the door, and the differences mount as the day progresses. While I consciously made a choice to have my life be a balance of work and home, the temptation to compare my life to yours is sometimes too strong to ignore.

For the purpose of this chapter, I'm going to establish two camps:

the working mama vs. the stay-at-home mama. While it may appear I'm making swooping generalizations of each camp, the examples and ideas are based on my own experience, my own perceptions, and my own demons. All that being said, I do believe that being a stay-at-home mom is the hardest job in the world, and sometimes the root of my own guilt for working comes from feeling like I took the easy way out by going off to work. Then there is more guilt because I actually enjoy it.

At some point, every mother faces the decision of what type of mama she will be—working or stay-at-home. Some make this decision before they even say "I do." For others, life happens, circumstances evolve, and when that plus sign appears, then they have to make this difficult decision. In my Christian community, a strong bias exists for the stay-at-home path. Some of these moms place heavy emphasis on homeschooling, homemaking, and caregiving within your four walls. It is easy to feel judged, even though you're among church people. When I express that I cannot volunteer for vacation Bible school on a summer weekday from 8:00 A.M. to 12:00 P.M., the response I typically get is, "Oh, you work?" Yes, I work. It's in this moment that I perceive the judgment, whether or not that is the intention. For so long admitting the truth that I worked outside the home felt like it required an immediate follow-up of an apology. I felt I had to overcompensate and explain details of our finances and conclude with, "But I have to work."

I believed this response to my core because when I found out I was pregnant we were a two-income household with a lifestyle built on both of us being contributors. I never looked at our situation as having another option. It didn't feel like the choice I was presented with was to work or stay home, I viewed the choice as have a baby now or wait. I believed that if I chose the now option it would require I work.

Recently I had a discussion about embarking on this book journey with a friend, Dayna. She asked me that question I had heard so many times before. When I gave my "I had to work" response, she lovingly challenged it. Did I really *have* to work? Isn't there always a way? There are plenty of people with lesser incomes who make this choice to stay home. She was lovingly challenging me to see that maybe my choice was rooted more in a desire to work than a need. I can think of no better time to shift my thinking on this topic than in the middle of writing a book for working mamas, because I think this is a very important part of our journey to soul freedom. The first step is admitting . . . I chose to work.

I am now able to look at the early years when Ella was born and own this truth: I didn't *have* to work, nor did I owe anyone an explanation about my *choice* to work. While the circumstances of our situation at the time of my pregnancy would have required drastic lifestyle changes in order for me to step away from my job, there was a way. There is always a way. We could have sold our house, moved in with family, shared a car, and had very little extra spending money. But I wanted so much more for us, and in full disclosure, I wanted to work. I loved my job. I loved the career path God had set me on. Growing up with a mom who worked, I realized you could be a good Christian, a good wife, a good mom, and still a good employee. I also wanted certain things for my kids that came easier with my choice to work. I wanted to be able to send them to a nice preschool, enroll them in extracurricular activities, create a college fund, and have annual Disney passes (priorities, right?). All of these things were a result of my choice to work. My intentions were not materialistic; they were about provision for our family and future to build a life full of experiences. I'll talk more about accepting that you can't have it all later in the book, but in this decision the sacrifices that would have allowed me to stay home far outweighed the benefits.

In the introduction, I talked about what I hope this book does for you. There are stories, anecdotes, and practical tips to help you create order in your chaos and begin to live your life unchained from guilt, apologies, and busyness. Yet we can do none of this if we live in the lie that our choice to work is a sin. We cannot keep that lie from replaying in our mind every time we walk into a group of stay-at-home mamas unless we balance it with truth, the truth found in the Bible.

At the creation of man, God made Adam to tend and work the garden. When He decided it was not good for man to live alone, He created Eve. What is so important to note here—and this might be new to you—is the intent God had for creating Eve: "Then the Lord God said, 'It is not good for man to be alone. I will make a *helper* who is just right for him'" (Genesis 2:18, author's emphasis). God did *not* say, "I will create a woman to make babies and be a companion." The very intention in the creation of woman was that she would work alongside of man. If that is not enough to get you to drop the apology for working, then flip to Proverbs 31, beginning in verse 10. The Proverbs woman is well-rounded. She cares for her home and her fields, and "she is energetic and strong, a hard worker" Proverbs 31:17. There's a long list of tasks she accomplishes and characteristics that give her the title "virtuous," and most are rooted in work.

To summarize this concept, Eve worked, and the Bible calls the woman who works for a profit the virtuous woman. Working mamas, can I get an amen! We have freedom in Christ, freedom to live outside of the legalistic ideas of not only the Old Testament laws but also some churches today. You have not just freedom to work a job, but right there in the black Times New Roman print of God's Word, you have His permission.

What do we do with this new idea of leaning into the gift and permission we have to go off to work? We live our own life according to the calling God has placed on us, but we do not alienate those with a different calling. We begin to see our stay-at-home mama sisters through a different lens and stop comparing. I like to define our differences as a "mom code," the set of guidelines and standards we set for our own parenting and the reasons that drive those convictions. We may live by a different mom code, but what time, maturity, and the good Lord have helped me realize is that we have the same goals. We are all approaching this motherhood thing with a two-part purpose: survive and thrive. We long to survive the hardest job we will ever do. And we want to thrive out of love for our children and the appreciation we have for God's entrusting them to us. Along the way to achieving these two goals, we can't help ourselves from comparing our tactics to the tactics of those around us. We can scrutinize and judge, and in our insecurities we can become abrasive in our defense of our own choices. Neither camp is exempt from these judgments, whether real or perceived, and as a result we fall into this trap of a lifetime of making excuses and apologies.

I've put together a mental laundry list of some of the hot topics that tend to divide us based on some of my own experiences with the other camp. I've been involved in a few daytime Bible studies and playgroups on my days off, and these typically pull in the stay-at-home mom (SAHM) crowd because of the time they meet. Sometimes there are one or two others who work part-time or from home, but I'm usually the odd one out. I'll be real with you, I don't feel like I fit in no matter how nice the SAHM women are or how much I crave friendship with other women. It's not because I don't love each one of them individually. I can have 1:1 friendships with these women like it's my second job, but during group time, that's where the code is so much different. They are there for support, to share their stories and vent their frustrations, many of which I cannot relate to. Some themes I've encountered over and over go something like this:

1. We don't do TV.
2. We don't do sugar.
3. We don't do electronics.
4. We don't do soda . . . ever. In fact it is probably the juice of the devil.
5. We don't go to McDonald's.
6. We don't give our kids our phones at restaurants. They color and sit like soldiers.

Some SAHMs express these opinions openly in bold proclamation, while others imply them by behaviors or pieces of conversations. Regardless of how they deliver their views, it's easy for us working mamas to feel judged if we differ in any of these areas. I have a tendency to perceive these statements as judgment based on my own demons from years of the self-imposed guilt that I allowed to fester from choosing to work. While God has brought me to a place of peace with my decision through the power of His Word, I still feel a need to explain it from time to time. These moms are all talking homeschooling, and I am talking public school plus at least two nannies to pick the kids up and shuttle them to their activities. All of those aforementioned "don't" items made it to that list because . . . I do them. My differing opinion is not exclusively on the basis of being a working mom; the truth is some of these choices are rooted in the fact that I have to choose my battles. I could justify them all day long, but I have found peace in my own motivations to allow room for those choices, even if they differ from the choices of other moms at playgroups. I'm learning to accept our differences because I am understanding more and more that our survival techniques are not built on the same foundation—back to our different mom codes. At the end of the day, the lifestyles of SAHMs and working moms are just plain different.

While we can speculate about the judging undertones of their mom code, perhaps their decisions have no judgment in them at all. The reality is, I wrestle with my own scrutiny of SAHMs that are equally unfair when I don't take time to understand their code, so I cannot be surprised when it comes back at me. The way to break the barriers that divide us on some of these hot topics is to understand the convictions that drive our decisions and find some common ground in theirs. The stay-at-home mom might actually be making her decisions based on something like this:

1. We don't do sugar . . . BECAUSE my kids turn into crazy people who bounce off the walls like squirrels trapped in a padded room and I have a solid eight hours to deal with them by myself before said sugar rush crashes and burns into quiet slumber.
2. We don't do TV . . . BECAUSE we spend a lot of time in this house and if we don't set boundaries for that, we will all end up spending our day in front of that box of mind-numbing mush.
3. We don't do McDonald's . . . BECAUSE we made a financial sacrifice to allow mom to stay home and with that came a commitment to be good stewards of our resources by not eating out. (I'm going to talk more about this topic of financial differences in the chapter on money because I think it's too important of an issue to gloss over. How God entrusts us with our money and the way we choose to spend it are such personal and individual matters in our relationships with Him, but one topic that seems to get so much hype and bring out such varying opinions is what Christian spending looks like.) Most families with a stay-at-home mama made a sacrifice financially

to afford that blessing. That's something we working mamas have to be conscious of as we compare our differences.

The list of potential justifications goes on and on, based on life, survival, and the desire to be in your place and do your mom job as unto the Lord. We working moms don't know SAHMs' true motivations any more than they know ours, but boy do we judge or feel judged because of differing opinions. Sometimes I find the need to explain our differences and either hide or apologize for my choices so much that it wears me out until I start isolating.

We explored in Chapter 3 that God created us for community, not isolation. Some of the very people I tend to isolate from are the ones whose company I enjoy the most, despite our differing opinions on Happy Meals. It doesn't matter if they view the golden arches as a Do Not Enter sign or if the first soda their kids taste is mixed with Jack Daniel's when they leave for college. We can accept and understand each other; we just have to show compassion and talk about the differences. With the power of the One who lives in us we can also choose not to judge. We can make every attempt to respect each other's beliefs and parenting styles with the best of intentions and yet still misstep on occasion. In those moments you have to be ready to just roll with it and accept it. Bear in mind that when those difference flare, neither camp needs to make excuses for their choices.

One day last year, Ella had a friend over after school. This was a new friend whose mom I had only met once, and we were having our very first play date. This play date was rolling over into our Awana program at church that night, so I decided we should do a quick run through McDonald's for dinner. I asked the little friend what she would like when we pulled up to the menu, and she took an unusual and curious amount of time to decide. As they each took their Happy Meals in hand, she unwrapped her cheeseburger and sunk her teeth into the first bite. She uttered these five earth shattering, ground-shaking little words I will never forget after she finished chewing: "I've never had McDonald's before." Could I be hearing her right? Did I just give this girl her first McDonald's ever at nine years old? She hadn't grown up in the African plains or the Sahara Desert. This clearly had been an intentional choice on her family's part, and I had just shattered it with one quick pass-through. As I saw the bliss on her little face, I felt compelled to say, "What happens in Miss Katie's car stays in Miss Katie's car." She winked, and I knew she got it. She wanted to savor this meal without fear of repercussion as much as I wanted to keep this hidden from her mama. Clearly we had different views on fast food, and I learned the lesson that from now on, if we were going to indulge in fast food of any kind with a friend in tow, I would ask them what their favorite place was so we could be sure not to step in that again! I may not subscribe to others' choices for raising their kids, but I always aim to respect them.

I am not some crazy mom who wants to raise 700-pound, McDonald's-frequenting, TV-addicted kids. We have boundaries and reasons for our choices too. Allow me to take a minute to tell you some of my "becauses" for our choices to help you understand me. This might get you thinking about formulating your own. Chances are that throughout your parenting journey you will find yourself in the position I have over and over again where a stay-at-home mama wants to *understand* your choices. Rather than diverting to aggressive defense, you'll be ready to have a conversation.

In our house . . .

1. We do TV . . . BECAUSE sometimes mama needs ten minutes to get dressed for work and we allow some TV screen time at periods that are most convenient for what I am trying to accomplish. Because my kids get frequent television time, TV is just a normal thing. They don't binge on it. I'd have to duct tape my kids to the couch to get them to finish a whole episode of a show or watch an entire movie. They watch a few minutes, then they get up and move to something else. It's not something they earn or try to sneak in; it's just there in the room, and it doesn't control us.

2. We do sugar . . . BECAUSE I grew up in a home where it was limited but available. Because of this, I never had a love affair with sugar. I learned that in moderation, like anything, it wasn't bad or damaging. We don't have candy every day by any

stretch, but on occasion, especially when we are on vacation, we may or may not have ice cream for breakfast. I can hand my kids a box of M&Ms or a bag of skittles at the movies and they will eat about a quarter of a serving and hand them back to me. Why this self-control at such an early age? Because sugar does not control us! We control the intake, and it's just a part of their life.

3. We do electronics . . . BECAUSE, let's be honest, there is an app for everything! Learn to read, learn multiplication, become an amateur photographer with a cell phone, or start a YouTube channel and become mini moguls. This last item is of particular interest to my kids. But we monitor, we control, and we time it. The timing usually works to the benefit of my schedule or situation. We do family dinners around our kitchen table every single weeknight with no devices present except maybe our Alexa playing some Christian music in the background. On weekends, if we go out to eat, we allow the kids to have electronics. This is for the benefit of anyone within eight tables of us, so we can all eat in peace.

4. We do soda . . . BECAUSE of the same reason we do sugar. It's a treat in moderation, typically at restaurants only. We don't buy soda and keep it in our house, but my kids have come to enjoy when they are out for dinner and can have a root beer. They get one kid's size before they have to switch to water. Meadow usually throws away almost three quarters of her kid's cup, and Ella knows her limits. If the waitress offers her a refill, she makes her own decision to say no thank you and ask for water. Soda's not great, no argument there, but we grew up with moderation in all things and it's what we wanted to pass on to our kids.

5. We've already established we do McDonald's (and apparently impress McDonald's on innocent others) . . . BECAUSE my kids are incredibly picky despite our many efforts to force them to eat new things but they like McDonald's. And in truth we mostly use it for those days we are busy, going from work to activity, church, or errand and getting home just in time for

bed and bath (because we do our best to always go to bed on time!). I've seen the great tip from other moms to serve up some healthy bento boxes filled with nuts, dried fruit, cured meats, and whole grain crackers when you are too busy to cook or are not going home between activities. I could certainly try to hand my kids one of these well-curated bento boxes, but I'm pretty sure I'd need to duck in cover because they would use the cured meat as a projectile. I'd rather them eat a hamburger, a yogurt, and apple slices than a granola bar and goldfish, so we do what works! We aren't patronizing the golden arches on a daily or even weekly basis, but when it's convenient and makes life a little bit simpler, we drive right through and leave our guilt at the curb.

There are a lot of other dos and don'ts, and the list of parenting choices that divide us could go on forever. What I've realized is most of the "really good choices" you see in your Pinterest feed or read in the pregnancy and parenting books, like eliminating all processed foods from your home, checking labels for GMOs, using cloth diapers exclusively, creating an agenda of activities rather than resorting to TV, and crafting a busy book or box for restaurant dining, take a ton of time and commitment. In order to make that level of commitment, you need to have conviction. My conviction runs deep with some things, and for those I take the time to put in the effort. As a working mom, it's not really possible to be that perfect mom who rids all processed foods, uses only cloth diapers, creates a daily agenda, and never allows TV. I have to make a decision to prioritize the choices that are important and dedicate time to the convictions that are my own, not those fueled by comparing my choices to those made by other moms.

For instance, I am committed to my kids having a full education experience. I expect them to perform to their potential, and I don't encourage them to miss school, short on their assignments, or pass up extra credit. I also want my kids to be well-rounded, so I have found one sport and a church activity for each of them. I want them to grow up to love Jesus, and I know that starts by experiencing Him young, so we commit to Awana, and we don't miss or skip it unless we are out of town. With Ella, I made my own baby food and only bought Pampers and natural diapers in her early years, and with Meadow I chose to settle for organic jarred baby food and we bought whatever diapers were on sale. I didn't love Meadow less or worry less about her health and wellbeing; I just had less time to focus on these matters. If it came down to spending my Sunday evening making baby food for the week ahead or using that time to play a game with Ella, I chose the game. In order to make those choices without feeling guilt or shame, I had to learn to check in with the motivation for those decisions.

Whether we work, stay at home, or are sitting with a round belly and have yet to meet our baby, we all want to love our kids and do the best job we can with this mom thing. We make the choices for our situations and form the convictions that we feel will have the greatest outcome. Our choices may be unique, and our lives may look different on the surface, but those differences shouldn't result in judgment or isolation from each other. I pray over this with angst. I want to be the change agent, to see the differences and celebrate them. I long to compliment the friend who does take the time to bake the organic bread on which she spreads her homemade, gluten-free, dairy-free almond butter rather than feel less-than or angry because she is trying to redefine this mom code in a way I just can't hang with. Chances are, she looks at some aspects of my life and feels the same insignificance, insecurity, or inability to measure up.

One person helped me understand this relationship between working moms and SAHMs and appreciate our similarities more than our differences, and that is my sweet cousin Noelle. She didn't start out as a stay-at-home mama. She was a teacher who gave so much to her students but felt a deep desire to be home. She made sacrifices to do that and jumped all in without looking back. There are differences in our mom code because to get through her daily routine she has to set boundaries and control the environment, the food, and the activities. Without structure and a schedule she can quickly find herself outnumbered, outsmarted, and in big trouble. She has to stay one step ahead and create activities, learning opportunities, and conversations appropriate for toddler- through elementary-age kids, all while juggling three different nap schedules and a household of chores.

Noelle showed me that for her to maintain order in her home (which is lovely, inviting, beautiful, and cozy) she has to work at this several times a day. There's a morning cleanup, afternoon nap cleanup, and bedtime cleanup. Little ones have the ability to pull every item off a shelf in record time and put it back . . . oh, NEVER. Noelle doesn't just have big toy boxes where it all gets thrown in; she maintains the same level of organization I do but has to work much harder at this. My house is clean 90% of the time because I cannot rest without some level of order and organization. It might be easy for the SAHM to speculate about how hard this is for me to maintain because I am so busy with work and the kids. I'll give you a behind-the-scenes secret: this is one of the easiest mom tasks I do. We aren't home all day, so I don't have to keep cleaning and re-cleaning messes made from seven to seven. One mama may look at my house through the lens of comparison and guilt because she doesn't have the same state of tidy, but she doesn't understand this is actually something that comes rather easily due to my work schedule.

Here we are, two different moms, two different mom codes, same goal, and it takes us such different approaches to achieve it. While it might be easy to keep my house clean, it is sometimes an act of supernatural power to be able to muster enough energy to play a round of chutes and ladders and pretend to be big sister to Barbie in the dream house after I get home from work. By contrast, Noelle carves out time to sit and really play with her kids. When it comes to finding time for our own interests, if Noelle wants a pedicure she has to use up one of her grandma favors or ask her husband for a break to be able to sneak away for an hour or so. I can often squeeze in a hair appointment or pedicure on my way home from work while my sitter is already on the clock. Noelle's work is her home, so she doesn't have the luxury of passing those places on her commute.

Because I have loved her so deeply for as far back as I can remember, having grace for Noelle comes easily. The temptation to compare and judge and measure up to her just passes by. It also helps because she gives me the courtesy of the same grace. She doesn't openly judge me when my kids immediately ask for an iPad in the car or order a soda at dinner. The way I have heard her explain our different preferences and choices to her kids is a result of us taking the time to really understand them.

Maybe you've already realized this, but not everyone is like Noelle. Some people are more passively judgmental or downright aggressive. I have known a couple of mamas to wear their opinions like badges of honor, completely unconcerned with whom they may offend by expressing them. Some people say things about you or to you that are plain hurtful. I'm sure it isn't too difficult for you to think of at least one incident in which you were on the receiving end of a hurtful comment because you are a working mama. It's hard to see a reason for a comment intended to make you feel like the worst parent in the world just for doing your very best.

There was one person in my life for a season that continuously and intentionally drew out our differences and tied them to my choice to work. Her name was Tammy. She did not intend to build me up in support or encouragement; she intended to put me down as a mom. I remember sitting with her over coffee and discussing my countdown to returning to work after having Meadow. I was sharing how God had answered our prayers for childcare and I was very optimistic about the sitter we'd found. Her response sucked the oxygen out of the room for a brief minute. As I struggled to catch my breath, I was also trying to figure out if I had actually heard her correctly. Her one ignorant comment had the ability to make me second-guess every decision I had felt so confident in just minutes before. It had that power, because I allowed it to.

"I don't know how you could ever entrust your baby to a stranger. That is why I quit my job when I had my kids," Tammy had said.

She didn't follow it up with an encouraging reminder of God's protection or any other qualification. In all of my replaying and rewinding of this conversation in my head, I can't come up with a single constructive reason why she would respond like this. Unfortunately, comments like this about my choice to work became regular in our conversations, and I began to slowly withdraw from our relationship.

After years passed and we were no longer in contact, I realized that this woman was hurting so much in her own life and was dealing with it by lashing out at me. She grew this canyon between us by calling out and magnifying my shortcomings. In God's love and mercy, He sometimes moves people out of your life for reasons only He knows, and that is exactly what I believe He did here by removing Tammy from mine. He also gave me some insight into these hurtful comments that had left me feeling broken and less-than for so many months. I learned through mutual friends that Tammy felt like she had left her identity with her job when she chose to stay home and was struggling to find purpose in her life as a stay-at-home mom. She had expressed to our friends that the greatest desire of her life was to have a job, contribute to their finances, and have something of her own. In her mind, I was living her dream. I didn't get noticeably upset when she pushed at me, and that is why I believe she kept coming back to dish out more. God allowed me to endure that trying friendship to help me learn that sometimes the differences others attack us for are the very things they see in us and envy.

I am often guilty of this myself. Take breastfeeding for example. I had a deep desire to do it well, and if you read Chapter 1, you know that didn't happen. To this day, when someone is struggling with it and looking for support I can be guilty of making a comment or two about just giving it up. Why? Because at the root of the issue I have envy; breastfeeding is the one big thing I couldn't master. It's silly, and I catch myself and apologize if I offend someone, but it is so easy to do. Even if you don't speak it, you can probably point to at least one time when you thought something negative like this too. In your own insecurities do you ever allow your human nature to get the best of you? I draw attention to this not to shame you, but to remind you (and me) that we are all sinners. We all fall victim to the temptation of comparison at one point or another, and recognizing this in ourselves may allow us to show a little more compassion to the offender when we find ourselves on the receiving end.

Ladies, give yourselves room to live out your "because" and other mamas room to live out theirs. If you want to live your life in a way that brings joy to your comparison-prone soul, try to recognize the difference between guilt and convictions and choose to live your own life based on your unique mom code. Develop a code that serves you and your family well. Love others, show compassion, and realize that those who make you feel the most judged may be the ones looking into your life and wishing the pieces they see were their own. We are all on the same team. There is no offense or defense; we are all just moms working hard to grow our little ones into people who will one day survive on their own. If they are Christian mamas in the other camp, this should be that much easier because we all report up to the same boss. Our God can help us overcome the divide the world puts between us. Just because one of us gets up and throws on her sweatpants and the other puts on a pair of slacks and pumps doesn't make either one bad or wrong. Don't isolate yourself from the "other mama." Embrace her and love on her and be real with her so that the pieces that look like such a dream in your life are not the only ones she sees.

Chapter 4 Application
Know your own mom code

There are certain decisions you make in your parenting that stem from your own convictions. Maybe these are not popular choices among your friends. Whether your playgroup moms, church friends, or work friends view you as the strict mom or the sugar mom who lets her kids do anything, you have arrived at your decisions based on some conviction. If you can think ahead of the awkward conversations and prepare some answers built in love and grace, those moments will be so much easier to bear. So take a minute and define your mom code.

The mom code

Parenting decision we allow:	Because:

Now take a moment to answer the following questions:

- What are the parenting choices that cause me to feel guilty around friends? Is this guilt of comparison or a conviction of my choice? If you can't answer that, pray for clarity.
- How may I be judging others because of their parenting choices?
    - Is my judgment rooted in jealousy?
    - How can I show love and grace in these situations?

Chapter 5

Taming Your Children: Parenting Takes Bucks, Bribery, and Surrender

To discipline a child produces wisdom, but a mother is disgraced by an undisciplined child.
Proverbs 29:15

I've been disgraced a time or two. One day after work, I picked up then four-year-old Ella from preschool and we stopped by Michael's craft store to grab some after-school craft projects. Ella had been talking about wanting to paint a birdhouse for days, and on this particular afternoon I had enough time to make this happen. As we browsed the birdhouse aisle her excitement was spilling over by way of diarrhea of the mouth. She was talking up a storm about all the colors she was going to paint the birdhouse, where she was going to place it in the yard when she was done, and how she planned to entice birds to enter into it with peanut butter and birdseed. She carefully selected an A-frame style with a single entry hole for her potential bird habitants. When I told her that Mommy needed to go up and down a few more aisles to get some other things, her mood shifted and she became very impatient and negative. By the time we rounded the corner to the checkout, I had given her several stern-eyed stares and reprimanded her more times than I could count. She stood by the register with her little arms crossed tightly against her chest and a scowl of epic proportion.

The cashier noticed her very unhappy demeanor and started to address her in a loving tone. "Aren't you just the cutest little girl! Is this your birdhouse?" And Ella abruptly answered, "Yes." "What do you plan to do to it, young lady?" the clerk asked. With that question Ella took about thirty seconds of silence to carefully ponder her response. She then delivered this atomic bomb that is a pivotal point of embarrassment in my motherhood career. Through pursed little lips she uttered these five words I will never forget: "Put it in my butt." I get the hysterical belly giggles just typing that and every time I recount that story now, but in that moment I was totally and completely mortified. I apologized profusely to the cashier, who seemed relatively unfazed by the comment, and I resisted eye contact as she rang up the remaining items for what felt like an eternity. When we got to the car and I asked Ella what on earth she was thinking, she couldn't even give me a response. We don't have to teach our children sin; it is ingrained in their nature. I can confidently say Ella never heard me tell anyone I planned to put something there, so she certainly cooked this one up all on her own.

Have you ever found yourself in a season of parenting in which the behavior your child is demonstrating is more like that of a wildebeest than the sweet angel baby you birthed? Have you entered the crazy zone where your day consists of yelling at your kids, crying to yourself about losing your cool, apologizing to them for losing said cool, losing all credibility because of the apology, and then yelling again when they repeatedly disobey? Or are you familiar with the thought *I cannot wait to go back to work* after a long weekend home? This feeling about home, like it's a place you can't wait to escape, rattles a soul longing for peace. Arguing with our kids to get them to cooperate and obey and raising our voices in frustration is guaranteed to heap on the mom guilt we have been working so hard to shred.

Working mamas have several extra struggles here, because first, we aren't raising our kids alone, and second, we are away all day and don't want to have to lose our cool in the few hours we have at night. Your kids likely spend as much time with a nanny, grandparent, teacher, or other caretaker as they do with you. No matter how thorough your instructions are on how you want your kids raised, the other people in your children's lives are all going to impact them in unique ways and make their own choices, which may not all line up with your priorities. When we go off to work, we hand the keys and instruction manual to whomever we are entrusting our children to and drive away praying they wont mess it up. We remind ourselves repeatedly that it is okay to go off to work, that work is not a sin, and that our kids will be just fine. Then we have a rough day, traffic is horrific, we spill coffee on our shirt on the way in, and nothing else seems to go as planned. When the kids are a little extra cranky and uncooperative and start to step out of line, we find ourselves back in the crazy cycle of losing our cool. Here comes the dump truck filled with guilt that speaks lies into our souls, like "How dare you lose your cool when you just got home?" and "You should choose your battles because you don't want to be the one person in their lives always yelling at them." There is a little truth to these statements (maybe we need to change our disciplinary tactics if we are losing it on the regular), but letting our kids get away with bad behaviors out of our guilt is not the answer.

After too many outbursts leaving me crying and guilt-ridden, I resolved that there had to be a better way to encourage positive behavior than losing my temper. Screaming is not discipline. I needed guidance for effective correction, so I went back to the Word for some direction. The Bible talks about disciplining our children out of love and obedience to God. I was failing to discipline out of corrective direction; I was choosing to yell and allow my anger to outburst because it was easier than crafting a plan and reinforcing positivity. I had cried too many tears of regret following the times I raised my voice and let the stress of the situation consume me. I had squandered my soul in the category of parenting. I decided I wanted to be the strongest force of influence in the guidance and direction my children received, even if their time was divided among other caretakers. In order to be that voice of influence they respected and sought out for guidance, I needed to draw them in with love and compassionate instruction rather than drive them away with yelling and a short temper. From my desire to make a positive change that would build structure in our home, Mom Bucks were born.

The summer between first and second grade for Ella was when

we first encountered our cycle of routine disruptive behavior and parental outbursts. From an early age she had developed an attitude and personality inclined toward sin and sticking birdhouses where they didn't belong. At the age of seven it was as if these traits hit a climax, and an incredible sense of entitlement and sass developed in her rapidly. We hadn't expected it; we didn't know what hit us.

Meadow was a year old and needing the bulk of our attention because the sole focus of parenting between the ages of one and two is keeping the child alive. This left Ella searching for her place in our schedule. Not only did she have a mom and dad who both worked outside the home, but the time that we used to dedicate solely to her was now shared with a tiny human who ate, slept, pooped, and cried . . . all the time. When our time was stretched and we prioritized by level of demand, as most kids will do, Ella clawed her way to the top of the demand list by acting out. Our patience was thin. We were adjusting to this new normal, and we yelled way more than we had ever wanted to. I would sit on the floor in my closet or outside their two rooms after they were both in bed and cry crocodile tears. I believed I was failing miserably at this parenting thing and felt I didn't deserve these two girls I had prayed so long and hard for. Sometimes at night after a tearful outburst or regrettable reprimanding, I would slowly turn the doorknob to their room and creep in on tiptoes to stand over them while they were sleeping. Their angelic little faces would be in the sweetest slumber, and I would watch their chests rise and fall with every breath. I would stand there and take in the magnitude of those breaths, each one a precious gift from God. These girls were my heart's greatest desire, and they were everything I had dreamed of and more. They were not naughty, malicious, evil children. They were two little girls born with a sinful nature, struggling for their mom and dad to guide them toward truth. Singling out the ways they were failing was not helping them understand their behavior, and it wasn't bringing any of us joy.

In my helpless state of worn-out shame, I started to give it over to God by getting on my knees and praying for a solution. I prayed God would give me patience. I prayed He would show me specific ways I could develop in them a desire for good. Then I did what all moms do these days: I googled it—"How to positively reinforce your kid so they want to behave." The sheer quantity of results (both secular and spiritual) was staggering. I found a small bit of comfort in knowing I was not the first mom to be in this predicament. I applied principles from various articles to develop a system that made a pivotal change in our parenting. We called it Mom Bucks.

The concept is simple and something you can relate to. You get up every morning go to a job you may not be thrilled about, you work hard and do your best because at the end of the week you are compensated. Your paycheck is your positive reinforcement that fuels you. Sure, more than money motivates you; I'm not suggesting we are all shallow. But chances are, if you woke up tomorrow and your job said there was no longer a paycheck but you could keep coming, you wouldn't show up. The money motivates us because the money supplies our wants and needs. It feeds our family, allows us to take vacations and indulge in our favorite things, and puts a roof over our heads.

I applied this concept to thoughts about Ella. What motivates her? What are her wants, and how could we turn her attitude of entitlement into one of workmanship and gratitude? The most important part of this process was engaging her in it from day one. We took a large chalkboard that hung in our hallway, sat together, and came up with a list of items and experiences Ella wanted to work for. Like all children, despite our best judgments and limitations, she lived for screen time. We recognized this obsession and wanted to limit it but still make a way for her to earn it through her own choices. Together, we developed a list of rewards that included the following items: screen time (thirty-minute increments), having a friend over, five dollars for the dollar store, a trip to Barnes & Noble for a new book, going to the splash park or community pool, spending the night at Grandma's house, fifty dollars and a trip to the American Girl store, a night out with Mom, a night out with Dad, and going to the movie theater.

Each item had an amount in Mom Bucks assigned to it. Screen time started at ten Mom Bucks per half hour, and the grand prize of a trip to the American Girl store with fifty dollars was 250 Mom Bucks. Once the rewards were set, we discussed the habits and behaviors that needed attention and made a list. The items consisted of chores, positive behavior choices, timed reading, etc., all of which would earn the fake money. If Ella did all the items on the list in a single day she could earn up to forty Mom Bucks per day. The kicker was, there were also things she could lose them on, like talking back to Mom or Dad, failing to do her chores, cheating on screen time—you get the idea. After we made our lists and she understood the system, we had her sign the bottom of the chalkboard, agreeing to the terms. We printed out five-dollar bills and cut them out together, and we hung up "Mom's wallet" and "Ella's wallet," which were made out of manila envelopes. Through this entire process she was so excited to be able to work toward a goal and earn things, some of which were very simple.

Once we were finished setting it up, Ella didn't even want to wait until the next day to start. It was as if we had flipped a switch and turned off the crazy cycle. From that point on, after school she would rush through the door and check her chart to understand where she stood for the day. Her first priority became her homework because it was a quick five bucks. Homework had been such a battle because we were used to an emotionless entrance into our home with an immediate desire to watch TV. She also tackled her chores and her reading before she even began to ask for privileges or spending. She would stand in that hallway with her bucks in hand, and she would just calculate and recalculate her options. She came alive and was motivated by this positive reinforcement. She set goals for herself each day and learned the value of spending and saving for what you really want.

Initially, she was all about the instant gratification. She would earn ten bucks, then immediately spend it on screen time. She realized this enjoyment wore off fast, though, and had to work pretty hard to earn another ten bucks. She stopped buying little things and started saving for the big-ticket items. It never ceases to amaze me that experiences are often more valuable to our kids than things. She would save for a night alone with Mom or Dad or a trip to the movies because she craved that time with us. It's so easy with two kids to forget that they each need time alone with us as much as we need it with them. When you get your kids alone, they become these incredibly cool individuals with whom you have meaningful conversation. As you juggle your career and home life, this is so hard to do. I totally get it. At the end of a long day, you don't want to not see one of your children or have a sitter come in or your husband keep one. You want to use the time you do have home to enjoy the company of all of your family members, but it is essential and so fulfilling when you make time for them individually (including your husband). You push pause on all of the craziness of life, and they are your world, even if just for a couple of hours. Carving out a system that forced us to take one-on-one time with Ella eliminated any excuses of being too busy with work, chores, or Meadow.

Despite the radical change we experienced, we had realistic expectations that there would be times this system would fail us. We are all born with sin and will struggle with it throughout our lives. So I can't say this cured it all. Ella still had slip-ups and disobeyed, but we stayed firm on our system. Having to reach into her little paper wallet and pay out the penalty of her sin was an event that always brought her to tears. She had worked so hard to earn those Mom Bucks, and she understood the setback of having to lose them.

One day this hit her hard because the penalty was great. Ella has always had an unnatural gift of sarcasm, and this would often get her in trouble. I don't remember the particular words exchanged that cost her that day, but I remember that her comments and tone of voice were disrespectful and inappropriate. She was close to the American Girl prize, and this slip-up set her back several days. When I asked her to take down her wallet and pay me fifty Mom Bucks, her gaze dropped to the floor and she began to sob. I could see her brokenness as she handed over those ten five-dollar bills. She was sorrowful in the depth of her own little soul.

As her shoulders shook with each inhale through sobs, I gently placed my hands on them and led her to the bottom step of our staircase to sit next to me. It was in this opportunity I was able to show her God's great grace and the picture of His love that covered the multitude of our sins. I sat on our bottom step with her as she cradled her little head in her tiny hands and told her a story she had heard many times before. I told her how Jesus gave His life so that we may have ours. I told her how His sacrifice was something we did not deserve, and I confessed to her that even Mommy was guilty of sin. It was in that moment that I chose to show her the grace God showed me, and I handed her back half of the Mom Bucks she had just paid over. Her tears of sorrow and regret became tears of joy as she thanked me for the offering she knew she was not deserving of. This real-life illustration of grace shed to cover our sins is what led Ella to her own decision to accept the sacrifice Jesus had made for her.

When we were living in the crazy cycle, I thought I was choosing the easy route. I would work all day, come home exhausted, and put little effort into discipline or encouragement. When Ella was good, it was good. And when she acted up, we would yell. But the reality was, she was a seven-year-old little girl with a sinful nature looking to her parents to define what her standards needed to be for her life. The response she had to the positive reinforcement, encouragement, and taking a little extra time to build her a goal and a program of rewards paid dividends. It gave me more energy than I had before because I wasn't battling her, my own emotions, and the enemy of our soul to just get through the day.

Our children need us to define our expectations for their behavior. They need boundaries and limits and rewards. They will test those limits, they will push fifty feet beyond the boundary, and they will fail and have regrets and make mistakes. But these young years are precious because they get to make all of these mistakes and do all of these things under our roof with us watching over them, picking up the pieces and protecting them from all of the influences of the world. As working moms with other influencers and caretakers in the mix, we need to be particularly dialed-in and present during the time we get with them. We learn by doing, and we get better by making mistakes and trying again. Moments in your children's lives when you can see the sin poke through and identify their need for a savior are divinely appointed opportunities—the ones God uses to point us to Him.

That day on the stairs with Ella, I could have dished out guilt and shame. I could have driven home how difficult it would be to regain those bucks and reach her goal and made sure her sadness was so deep she wouldn't want to do it ever again. But God spoke to my heart; He showed me that her remorse was real and her heart was in pieces.

There is only One I know who can so graciously put those pieces back together, and I was able to introduce Ella to Him that day.

That summer when we came up with Mom Bucks, God used disobedience, exhaustion, and failure to shape our family. He used those failures for His good and showed us a way we could break the cycle and begin to foster a love and understanding for who He is in the life of our little girl. Our children don't want to hear the negative any more than we do. They don't want to show up and do their best only to be cut down because no one ever outlined for them what the picture of obedience looks like. We criticize their faults and poor behavior because we know it is our job to do so, but because we are busy and preoccupied with work and have such high expectations, we often forget to supplement with encouragement and positivity in between. As Christian women, it's hard to remember that the Spirit within us giving us discernment and keeping us from temptation is not inherent in their nature. This is a choice they have to come to on their own, and the way we can pull them into that choice and draw them near to our Savior is by painting a picture of a loving God who is worth getting to know. Who we are to our kids, how we talk to them, coach them, and teach them, is our testimony. Do we live our lives in such a way that they see something they are missing? Do they see a love and a joy and a peace that are outside of human comprehension? Or do they see a mommy who is tired and cranky and quick to run back to work?

We could have just set up a traditional allowance system, but at seven years old, Ella was too young to understand the value of money alone, so we looked for things she did value. Whether you try it our way or have a system of your own, find what your kids love and incentivize it. It may create limits around technology and other distractions that keep your kids from being kids. Ella played outside and used her imagination more that summer than any other. She was happy, excited, and filled with joy each time she reached a new limit. She took great pride in collecting her bucks at the end of each day and piling them up in her wallet. It was such a success in our home that we kept the system through the entire next school year. We changed some of the chores and prizes to keep it new, exciting, and relevant to the school year, and its effect never wore off. The impact was so strong I am writing an entire chapter about it!

There are hundreds of books on parenting out there written by scholars and doctors and people much smarter than I am, but as we already established, few are written by working moms. This was the impact we needed in the trenches of real-life parenting with a schedule that is complex and home time that is stretched thin. The version of myself who often ended her day with tears of regret knew there was so much more to this calling of being a mom. Our calling is about eternity and using the trying moments to win our children's hearts for Christ. Raising them in a home where they are exposed to Christianity is not enough to guarantee they will choose this path. As parents, we are their first example of Jesus lived out in flesh, and by our actions we will either draw them in or push them away. Our children are watching our every move and hanging on every word. If you don't believe me, just let one tiny little four-letter word slip in their presence. They will then find the most inopportune moment to pull that out of their word bank and use it in a scene that will leave your mortified.

There is no better place to practice what you preach than in the walls of your own home. As the character Spider-Man often says, with great power comes great responsibility. You are entrusted in a position of power the moment your children enter the world. You are their protector, their caretaker, and their provider. There is immense responsibility in this calling because we are now accountable to these tiny humans looking to us to show them what is right. We need to live out the truth that God is a god of compassion and love. We can show our children the picture of His mercy that is new every morning for you and me. But it's not enough to just show our kids grace; we need to explain it to them in a way that their little hearts can comprehend.

The Mom Bucks were just one tool God gave me to reset the temperature of our parenting that opened the door to so many other opportunities. I still mess up—ALL the time. I still cry on the stairs or in my closet on days when I lose my cool. Ella still sins even with the Spirit within her, and Meadow is following right behind. Not every parenting issue is going to have a quick resolve with a reinforcement system. We have learned in some battles with Meadow that not all kids will respond the same. We went through a season when she decided she hated preschool and cried hysterically every day for two weeks at drop-off. I applied the same research and positive reinforcement methods without any immediate success.

During this preschool season, I blamed myself for doing something to cause my child to respond this way. I told myself that if I were a stay-at-home mom I would feel so much less pressure. Maybe I could take the time each morning to ease her into the routine, spend a morning in the classroom, be at every drop-off and pickup, and, if we just needed a cuddle day, take more of those with ease. School would be that fun thing Meadow would get to do a couple of hours a morning to get her out of the house rather than the lifeline to get me to my job on time. I know some of this is false thinking because I have talked to many stay-at-home moms with the same separation issues and their cases were no easier. But when you are in the thick of crisis it is so easy to look around, compare, and build up the idea that you've got the toughest challenge on the planet. In the heat of those moments it felt like that to me. A stay-at-home mama doesn't have to call her boss to say she is running late for a mandatory meeting because her little one is holding on so tight to her car seat that it might take surgery to remove it. That was my reality. Every morning battle at drop-off meant I was running behind for a meeting or a call or some other work commitment. And every time it disrupted my timing and schedule, I had to make a humiliating call to say I was running late

The solution did not come easy. The morning I accepted that we were her parents and we knew what was best, we did the difficult task of letting her cry. The tears started flowing down Meadow's cheeks the minute we pulled in the driveway, and she began to wrap her arms and legs around anything she could use to secure herself. I parked, pulled her out with the force of wrestling an alligator, and brought her inside with tears and screams and arms flailing. The director met me at the door, gently pulled her off of me, and said, "Mom, we've got this."

The two-minute walk to my car was the most agonizing 120 seconds of my life. I sat in my car and audibly spoke these words: "Lord, I need you. I am out of ideas and don't know where to go from here."

I could not fix this situation with a chart or internet research. We had to let the tears flow, do the tough-love thing, and allow God to transform this experience into one that brought joy and excitement to Meadow's little heart. When I picked her up from school that day, her words were a reminder of exactly how great He is. Any evidence of the tears that marked her face that morning had long been dried, and she said to me, "I love school. I wish it were dark out so I could go to bed and wake up and be at school." I literally looked around the car and in every mirror to see if I was on some sort of hidden camera or if this was the world's worst idea of a joke. This transformation was so radical I could not believe it.

I didn't exactly understand, and I couldn't explain it or reason it, but day after day, she has continued to have the same anticipation and reaction. We had left those tears at the door on that tormenting morning. I am not a fool to believe or expect we will never have another bad day or tears at drop-off. I probably will feel all the same guilt and despair when and if it happens again. For those moments, I am writing it down now as a reminder to myself (and to you) that when we finally surrender and hand it over to God, He can take it, shape it, and make it new. He's done this in my own life, in my marriage, and in my parenting.

As our kids get older, the job seems to get more complicated. Kids are brutal in their judgments and quick to point out differences. At ten years old, I see Ella's daily battle to stand up for what she believes in. At times I see her hang her head in defeat because her choices aren't the same as the masses'. It is in those times I have to step in with loving guidance to point her back to a concept so difficult for her fifth grade brain to comprehend: this world is not our home. We have already encountered friends cursing, talking about alcohol, and imparting their own ideas about sex. I pray daily that God will give me the wisdom to tackle these challenging issues in a way that will stir in Ella and Meadow the desire to walk in God's will, but I know this won't always be easy.

I am not in the trenches of parenting a teenager yet, but what I do have to offer you is the testimony of my own teenage years to guide you if this is where you are at on your parenting journey. The testimony I am about to share with you is not about me at all; it is about He who is within me. So I pray you do not see this as a prideful display of all of the perfect choices I have made. Rather, I pray you view it as hope that in this broken world our children can stand out.

When I was fifteen years old, on my first day of tenth grade, I sat next to a boy I had known only by name and reputation. In the late Nineties, we would refer to a boy like this as "hot" or "fine." When he leaned over to introduce himself to me, my palms were immediately sweaty and my heart began to race. He was a varsity football player. Everyone knew at least his name, and here he was leaning over to talk to me! I like to think I was cute enough in those days, but I was by no stretch the popular girl. I was smart and focused on my studies, and as of this point in tenth grade; I had never been on a real date or introduced my parents to a boyfriend. At first, we became friends, and eventually we started to talk on the phone. In those early conversations I proclaimed who I was: a Christian, a virgin, a non-drinker, and someone who wasn't exactly looking for a serious relationship, especially with someone who did not possess those same qualities. I had heard the sermon a hundred times over about being equally yoked, and I made a decision at a young age to guard my heart from people who didn't, at a minimum, share my faith.

He was Catholic, and his family went to church regularly, and although he didn't oppose my beliefs in God, he lacked a relationship with Him. I don't think he believed me when I said I would not fall for someone who didn't share my values. We casually group dated in the presence of other friends, and then as a way to see each other outside of school he started coming to Young Life with me and eventually to my church on Sundays. Somewhere in those weeks when we were getting to know each other, God reached the depths of his soul and he found his own relationship with Christ. It wouldn't be long before he invited his entire family to our non-denominational church, and all of those values I shared with him on those early phone calls became his own convictions as well. After months of growing in a friendship and a relationship built on a new foundation, we became an official couple on February 14, 1999. I was fifteen years old, but there was not a doubt in my mind that what I felt for him was real love. This boy would later become my husband, Chris.

Remember how I told you my dad packed my lunch every day? Well, on one particular day in my sophomore year of high school, he was very concerned that I keep my lunch box by my side. At first I brushed it off and almost placed it in my locker, but then I remembered his words on my way out the door: "Please don't lose your lunch today." I carried it with me from class to class, and when I finally got to lunch and opened it, I was shocked to see a royal-blue velvet jewelry box inside. I slowly opened that box to reveal a dainty platinum band with a small emerald-cut diamond. My parents had written a card that said, "Katie you are more precious than rubies or diamonds. This purity ring is a reminder to always treat yourself as precious as you are." When my parents could see that Chris and I were serious in our feelings for each other, my dad purchased a purity promise ring that I wore on my left hand until my wedding day. This wasn't just a promise to my parents; this was a promise to God, and the ring was a physical reminder of that. That afternoon when I got home from school, I called my dad just like I did every other day, and the minute he said hello, I said, "Dad, I lost my lunch box." To this day we still laugh about it, and when I removed that ring on December 14, 2003 to replace it with my wedding ring, it went back in that blue velvet box where it will sit until Ella brings home her first boyfriend.

I had many people criticize the depth of my relationship with Chris, including parents of some of my closest friends. They saw us together often and witnessed Chris being invited on our family vacations. They knew he played football and was part of the "in crowd," and they made assumptions about our relationship and who I was as a person. I would try to defend myself, but the reality was, some of my friendships could not survive this pressure. One particular set of parents started a rumor at their church that my parents allowed co-ed sleepovers because on occasion, if Chris's mom was out of town, he was allowed to stay at my house—in the guest room, with my parents present. My parents were not condoning behavior that was outside of God's will for our lives. Instead, they decided to be present and part of our relationship. They wanted to know Chris intimately in order to be able to make their own decision about whether he deserved my hand in marriage someday. They wanted to be an influence in our lives and our relationship, and they became some of our best friends.

I watched so many of the parents of friends not take this level of interest in their dating relationships, and some even tried to forbid dating. Not a single one of those tactics were any more effective than the road my parents took. Sure, I could have rebelled, I could have taken advantage of their trust and the freedom they gave me, but the thing about extending trust is that the person granting it always knows there's a chance it will be abused. My parents rarely told me not to do something. In fact, when we had the alcohol discussion in high school, the directive from my dad was never to drink and drive. He promised I could always call him without repercussion, but the truth was, I knew having to ever make that call would be immensely disappointing. I never saw them drink, so I never drank. I had more freedoms and privileges than any of my friends, and that was not something I wanted to give up on a few bad choices.

Now in my adult years, I share this story with friends who have teenagers, and the first rebuttal I often get is, "Katie, times were different." That may be true to some extent, but even then every single one of my friends drank at parties at some point. Less than a handful of them graduated high school with their virginity intact, and on more than one occasion, each of them participated in a co-ed sleepover their parents had no idea about. Even though we were not phone-addicted, we had instant messenger and email and still hid behind those things in exchange for actual human interaction. The time was different, but so many of the issues were the same. I faced pressures every day, and I was not exempt from the desire to fit in.

I heard a powerful sermon on parenting a teenager delivered by my pastor, David Whitten. He spoke about the teenage years being an opportunity for our children to make their own decisions based on the guidance we give them. Pastor Whitten encouraged that we cannot parent a teen the same way we parent an infant or a preschooler. They no longer need us to tie their shoes, dress them, or interfere in their schoolwork and social activities. Our job is to be present while we allow them to begin to do life on their own. We are not in every aspect of their business, but we are available to redirect their path when they get off course. If we try to parent a teen the same way we do a younger child, we are insulting their intelligence and failing to prepare them to get into the real world. Your teenagers need some freedom to exercise what you have taught them, to make decisions, and maybe even to make some mistakes along the way, all under the tutelage, guidance, and safety of your watching eye.

Pastor Whitten isn't the only one to pioneer this philosophy for parenting your teenagers. A free resource for parents that my own parents often turned to for guidance and support is Focus on the Family. On Focusonthefamily.com, if you type in the word *teenager* in the search field, hundreds of results will populate your screen and provide you biblical truth to tackle even the most difficult issues. They draw first from the Bible and then from works by various authors and experts on the topic. I found many resources supporting the type of parenting that shifts from telling teenagers what to do to teaching them how to think for themselves. Extending freedom is the only way to allow for our kids to learn from their mistakes, and when done right, with God at the center, we can guide them back to the truth.

Perhaps you have been trying this and your teenager has abused the freedom and you are struggling to regain control. Maybe you are not meant to go at this alone. Help can be found in so many different forms. It can be a coach your child respects, a pastor, a life coach, or a youth counselor. At this age, no offense to you, but your teens are probably going to be more likely to follow the direction of another adult they respect than your direction. They are so easily influenced and often afraid to disappoint people they hold in high esteem. You are their parents. You have to love them, and chances are they know it. And maybe just like seven-year-old Ella acting out for attention, they are going through their own internal battle that has nothing at all to do with you and they need to feel your unconditional love and firmer guidance from someone else.

You may be a mama whose child has gone astray. If you are reading this and feeling nothing but a pit of despair because you feel you've done everything you can in your own strength, I want to encourage you. The free will of your child has led them down a path you cannot control. If your child is lost to drugs, alcohol, premarital sex, a gang, or something worse, I know your heart is broken in a million little pieces. In all of your parenting wisdom and unending love, you long to scoop them up and save them, but sometimes the hardest decision we have to make is to release them and practice faith. God can bring them back. I have seen it in countless lives of my friends and their children. This may be the greatest battle of faith you will ever have to fight, but iron sharpens iron, so go out there and connect with other parents who have been through it. But for the grace of God go I, it could have been you or me who made those choices. God can take the broken, lost sheep and He can lead them back. If this is you I think you need to hear this loud and clear: **mama, you are not the shepherd.** Jesus is, and He promises to never leave or forsake even one of His sheep. He leaves the ninety-nine. So let Him scoop up your lost sheep and lead them home while you rest in Him.

We can live in fear of our kids' teenage years. We can even utter things like, "I'm afraid to bring kids into this crazy world." But I find hope in Jesus' words in Matthew 10:34: "Don't imagine that I came to bring peace to the earth! I came not to bring peace but a sword." There are no surprises to the One who created this earth; He anticipated the crazy world we are living in long before we took our first breath. While Jesus can bring peace to your soul, this world will only get more unsettling because this is not our home. The sword that Jesus is bringing is what separates the holy from the unholy. We just need to decide which side we want to be on. We can do our very best, make decisions based on our prayer life, and show our kids, not tell them, how much freedom there is in Christ. As I look back on my own teenage years, I know they could have gone a million different ways. One little mistake or one different turn could have given me a very different story to tell, but I believe God protected me because the Holy Spirit was alive in me.

I know Ella and Meadow will make their own mistakes. They may not feel the same convictions I did or choose the same path. They may not meet boys who respect their desire for purity, and they may not choose to wear a ring that represents it. They have free will, their own desires and will be led astray by their own temptations. I could live in fear of all of the choices they could make that are outside of my control, or I can choose to play the role of influencer and hand the rest over to God. The best any of us can do is go back to the Word as our guidebook for daily encouragement. We can fill our minds with truths and defend our beliefs and convictions so when they ask us why we don't live like the rest of the world we know exactly how to answer.

No one has ever accepted something as truth just "because I said so." The kids today are far more intelligent as a result of the world of information at their fingertips. If we do not point them to truth, they will find their own truth. If we don't live by our own convictions and expect them to, they will see right through the hypocrisy and choose the same sin. If we live in defeat, throw up our hands, saying, "They will drink anyway," or "They will experiment with sex no matter what I say," and commit to just teaching them how to do it responsibly rather than creating in them a desire for holiness, we cannot be surprised when those are the exact decisions they make. There are very few sources they can go in order to be reminded they are fearfully and wonderfully made. It is our job as their parents to define for them what their lives are worth, demonstrate that they are more precious than rubies and diamonds, and point them to the love and grace that covers the multitude of their sins.

We cannot parent alone, especially as working moms, and we cannot expect with our finite minds and human nature to have all the answers. We are as sinful as our children, and the stress of daily parenting and trying situations mounts in us just as it does in our little ones. We will get it wrong so many times, especially when we solely rely on our own strength. Like with all lessons in life, God tends to meet us in our brokenness because that is when we are in a posture of surrender and need Him most. If you are a stressed out mama because parenting, molding, and shaping the lives of the kids God has entrusted to you feels like too big a burden to bear alone, you are exactly right. It is! Trying to do it all with just your own strength is a fast way to darken your soul. So lean into Him, give Him the keys to the minivan that carries your family through each day. Trust that He can meet you on the stairs of your home as you direct your child's heart through the acceptance of salvation, or in the halls of a preschool when you aren't sure if prayer or an exorcism is what the moment calls for. It's always prayer, it's always faith, and it's always He who can show up and radically transform the trenches of parenting so that you can do it with a soul on fire.

Chapter 5 Application
Your family mission statement

Does your house have a mission statement? Is there a set of values and principles you have decided on together? Are your kids aware of your goals for your home and lifestyle? If you took an inventory of the state of your physical space and the tone of your home, would it align with the mission of your family?

The Atmosphere: Your home is your sanctuary; it is your escape from your job, your schedule of activities, and the crazy world we live in. Your home is the place you can be yourself, find rest for your soul, and build your family. This is as much about the environment as it is the people in it. Use the following guide to begin to define for yourself what you want your house to look like.

When you think of your home as a welcoming sanctuary, what sights, sounds, and scents come to mind?

- **Sights:**
- **Sounds:**
- **Scents:**

Use those attributes to develop a description of your ideal space.

Example: I need my home to be free from chaos. I set a nightly tone of relaxation by cooking dinner to the sound of Christian music flooding the room from our Alexa. The scent of my favorite candle or essential oil mixes with the aroma of dinner. I have shed the skin of my professional attire in exchange for my favorite leggings and flowing cardigan. I am barefoot and my hair is pulled back, and all jewelry but my wedding rings is removed. For the first time all day, I feel like I can breathe. This is my space, this is my domain, and I am finally at home.

The People: Identifying the characteristics that define your family will allow you to have a visual reminder of your end goal. There are no perfect people, just works in progress. Laying out the traits that you strive to represent will give you a narrow focus for the way you raise your children and influence their character.

What words come to mind as priorities for the following:

- **Attitude:**
- **Affection:**
- **Attributes:**
- **Affirmations:**

Combine those words into a mission statement that you can share with your family and post in your home as a daily reminder of what this life is all about. I didn't leave you lines in this book because I want you to get creative with how you display this. Engage your family in creating something that can be displayed on the walls of your house.

Example: **In this house, we do:** forgiveness, mercy, second chances, third chances, hugs, snuggles, kisses, truth-telling, dinners around our kitchen table, prayer, sacrifice, service, loud singing, big dancing, dreaming, love, and a lot of laughter. **We do not:** hold grudges, blame others, rely on our own strength, gossip, disrespect with our words or actions, discriminate, give up, or do harm.

Chapter 6

Swapping Self-care for Soul-care: Ditching the Expectations and Entitlement

*And what do you benefit if you gain the whole world but lose
your own soul? Is anything worth more than your soul?*
Matthew 16:26

As working mamas we are told to wear our work as a badge of honor and to pull out a measuring cup to ensure our work life and home life have an equal balance. We are told that in order to take care of the ones we love we must put ourselves first—kill it at our jobs and prioritize our own physical, emotional, and mental health above all else—in a schedule that is already pressed to the max. We are told this is self-care and reminded that we deserve this. It was after several months of being led by these lies and running ragged in this hamster wheel of self above all, that I took a step back and thought, *Where does my husband fit in? Where are my kids in this? And most important, where is God?*

Self-care is a topic that is spreading like wildfire. Every blog, Instagram feed, and mom book all seem to repeat this same message to us. You see photo after photo of women partaking in activities like yoga classes, bubble baths, shopping trips, and fancy dinners, all with the hash tag "self-care." When I heard this phrase it did not sit well with my soul, so I tried to dissect the concept to understand why it came with so much guilt. I discovered that I do not disagree with the concept of taking care of our bodies, minds, and spirits. I simply disagree with the label and the motivation behind the movement.

During an Internet deep dive, I encountered countless results describing the phrase *self-care* that I have summarized into my own words to give us a working definition:

- If you are busy and stressed, it is *because* you are missing self-care.
- If you want to have a balanced life, simply apply self-care.
- If you want to let others know that you are important, elevate your needs above everyone else's.

This is what the world says about the motivation and the benefit of this movement. Now let's line this up with what the Bible says on the topic. Brace yourself. This may hurt a bit. In Philippians 2:1–11, the apostle Paul is speaking to the Philippians about what Christian living should look like, and he uses the life of Christ as the paradigm. Verses 3 and 4 are where the text really hits on this concept: "Don't be selfish; don't try to impress others. Be humble, thinking of others as better than yourselves. Don't look out only for your own interests, but take an interest in others, too." Ladies, there is just no way to sugarcoat that putting ourselves above others is *not* the key to balanced living. When we look at the life of Christ as our model for perfect living, it is easy to see that nothing in His life was about selfish intentions; it was about valuing others.

This truth does not command that we live a life of complete servitude with no rest and reprieve for our own bodies. God made provisions for that from the begging of creation, and Jesus lived this out with His own earthly life. When you move past the label, the act of caring for oneself encompasses all good things—getting enough rest, drinking enough water, and feeding your mind and your body with nourishment. There is hope for us to embrace this concept in a way that is fulfilling, restful, and guilt-free if we can shift our thinking to be kingdom-focused. Let's start by looking at our body. The Bible tells us in 1 Corinthians that our body is a temple of the Holy Spirit: "Don't you realize that your body is a temple of the Holy Spirit, who lives in you and was given to you by God? You do not belong to yourself" (6:19).

Would you throw trash in a temple? Would you forget to wipe mud off your shoes on your way in? Would you eat food and spill drinks on the floor? Would you stick gum under the pew (okay, guilty of this one a time or two!)? Chances are, the answers are no, no, and more nos. A temple is the house of God, and it is holy. You silence your cell phone, brush your hair, put on your Sunday best (denim if it's one of the contemporary churches), and have a reverence and respect for the house and its Owner. Like the physical temple and place of worship, your body is the dwelling place for the Holy Spirit. If you take time to meal prep, exercise, have routine physicals, and drink plenty of water, this isn't self-care at all. This is **soul-care.** This is an act of obedience, of worship, and of serving God with this physical body that is on loan to us.

I think this is the easiest command for us working moms to neglect. When we have worked and need to muster up energy to be with our kids at the end of a long day, taking time for our physical bodies can feel like a selfish luxury. As we shift our thinking to soul-care, however, we can accept that finding the time is actually an act of obedience. With that mindset, I encourage you to make time for your temple. There are so many ways you can do this with your family, and it will not feel like a sacrifice. It can be as simple as a family walk at night, a trip to a playground where you turn a game of tag into twenty minutes of cardio, or investing in a few dance exercise videos and making it a family affair with lots of giggles! You can make a family chart where you track your water intake and turn it into a contest and involve your kids in the meal prep so that you have more homemade meals than take-out. Like with all things, there is balance and conviction that can help you guide yourself in your motivation. After all, God knows if you get up and go to the gym or run six miles because you are caring for your temple or because you want to look like the girl on the front of the magazine, and you know it too. I have given up on the idea of the perfect body, but I have learned to embrace treating mine as the temple that it is. If caring for your physical body is now viewed as an act of soul-care and an act of obedience, how can you possibly carry any guilt with that?

Soul-care goes beyond our physical bodies. The word *soul* might not be something you use in everyday conversation. You probably don't encounter people at work or home and say, "How's your soul today?" But the truth is, we've all got one. It is the part of us that lives on when we shed these earthly bodies for the heavenly. On this side of heaven, it represents who we really are, what we think, what we feel, and what makes us so unique. As Christians, we often refer to our soul in the heavenly context because that is what we have been taught lives on for eternity. But how often do we stop and think about our current soul state? We spend time with our emotions and our thoughts, but how much are we investing in our earthly souls?

If we want to figure out a way to drop the working mom guilt for good, the only way to get there is to drop what the world tells us we should be doing and replace it with what is written in the Word. This world we live in is making deposits into our souls every minute of every day. When we let down our guard and allow those deposits to filter through our minds and penetrate our souls, it has the power to disrupt our joy and alter our path. As working mothers, some of those deposits tell us we need to aim higher, make more money, pass up our male counterparts, and live out the freedoms others have fought to give us in the workplace. This world feeds us lies and delivers empty promises. The lies produce a fleeting happiness that keeps us in constant search of something to quench our deepest thirst for purpose. Although we will not find true soul fulfillment until we are face-to-face with Jesus, it can be well with our soul this side of heaven.

What does a "well soul" look like? It looks like a woman who chooses joy, praises Him even in the midst of a struggle, and guards her heart from the lies of this world. It looks like a mother who knows her convictions and places value on what brings lasting joy, even if it means there are some sacrifices to be made in her career.

Your soul does not belong in a prison of mom guilt because you are a working mama. Your soul does not belong enslaved to unmet expectations for how your life should look or entangled in a web of comparison and selfish intentions. It does not need to invite in every lie the world feeds about how you should work and parent and where your ambitions should lie. What your soul does need is daily nourishment of truth found by time spent in God's presence and His word to keep your mind and heart sharp. Only then can you begin to recognize the efforts of the enemy to derail your joy and pull you into his pit of disappointment.

Who's this enemy I speak of? The Word says clearly that our enemy, the devil, prowls around like a lion looking to destroy his prey. He is real, and he is after us all. One of the greatest ways he can destroy your joy is by getting in your mind and convincing you that you are not living the life and getting the things you "deserve." In the life of a working mama the enemy has so much material; he has all of our work and all of our home lives at his fingertips. He can feed lies about how you should be advancing in your career, how that co-worker who doesn't work nearly as hard as you seems to keep getting the recognition, or how your husband doesn't help at home as much as your friend's husband does. Regardless of the specific lie he chooses, the root is typically grounded in some level of expectation and entitlement.

The minute you own the fact that you are a mama who chooses to work, the world imprints a set of standards and expectations for what your life should look like. It is conditioning us to believe we deserve something for this sacrifice. It is preaching that we must buy into self-centeredness. And it is lying.

When we focus on self above all else, we become enslaved to the expectations that take root. Mama, please don't waste precious time in the prison of what you think you deserve. There's freedom from that in Christ. Maybe it's your job, your boss, your kids, or your husband you are thinking about right now. Maybe you're saying, "That all sounds great, but, Katie, you just don't get it. You don't know my husband and how he fails to help and meet my needs," or "You don't understand the demands of my job, I have worked hard, and I deserve a break." I have been guilty of these expectations, and I have put so much pressure on myself to seek what I believed I deserved. When I finally took the time to get that deserved pedicure or shopping trip, though, the satisfaction fell short because it was riddled with guilt.

Freedom and joy are not found in expectations and entitlement. In fact, those are a prison. Whether it's a girls' night out, "me time," perfect kids, a promotion, a date night, or a weekend away with friends, falling into the trap of "deserving" is a slippery slope of self-destruction. The honest-to-God, Bible-based truth is, what we truly deserve is death, and through the undeserved sacrifice on the cross, we were given life. If you are a God-fearing, Jesus-loving woman, then you already know this is truth. You know that while we were still sinners, Christ died for us. We didn't do a single thing to earn or deserve that. If the stirring in your soul tells you putting self above others does not sit well, it is because of this truth: we deserve nothing.

The fact that we are undeserving does not mean that God has not made provisions for us to delight in our desires and enjoy pleasures of this life. Is there something that you know brings satisfaction to the depth of your soul but that your current reality doesn't make time for? When that is the case, it is easy to let disappointment take root and spread like a bad case of weeds. Rather than let those weeds choke out the beauty in your life, though, take an inventory of your time and identify a place where you can get back the things you love. By intentional planning you can determine how to get more of what you love by giving up some things that feel like a waste. This is not a list of self-care items; we already established that type of mentality isn't going to give us freedom to experience the loves of our life guilt-free. This is where we build our soul-care plan.

This exercise may not be a new concept, but nevertheless I encourage you to grab a pen and flip to the last page of this chapter to follow along. We are going to list out the things you love in one fluid list. This list of loves is intended to reach into your soul to define your desires. The items aren't all spiritual in nature; they are the blessings that connect you with God because you are thankful and you praise Him for giving you the opportunity to enjoy them. God created us unique but also in His image, so I love to find comfort in knowing there is a tiny bit of God that enjoys a *Better Homes and Gardens* magazine and a good pedicure as much as I do!

Hopefully we can all agree we love God, our spouses, our kids, and our family. This isn't an exercise in *who* you love. We did a solid job of tackling that in examining the bull's-eye of your village. This is an exercise in *what* you love. What things would you like to make more time for to enjoy and count as blessings, not anticipating them as expectations? For example, **I love the two hours at night when my whole house is asleep** and I'm awake alone to command the remote and catch up on shows, read a book, browse Pinterest, or in this case write. I am a night owl by nature, so I come alive between the hours of 7 P.M. and 12 A.M. What do I give up to indulge in this simple pleasure? Early mornings with a quiet house and cup of coffee before we start the day. Knowing in advance I have to make this trade-off, I pack lunches at night, organize what we need for the next day, and even pack my car before I go to bed. I know you might be thinking, *Why do I need to give this up? Can't I have both—two hours at night and early mornings?* Well, yes, you could. And I could, except this brings me to my second love.

I love sleep. Deep, uninterrupted, ten to twelve hours of consecutive sleep is one of my greatest pleasures. I feel like it's been nine years, eleven months, and sixteen days since I saw that kind of sleep, but a girl can dream. Early in life I learned to get ready in thirty minutes or less so I could maximize the number of times I hit snooze. I've managed to translate this into motherhood even with waking kiddos and a job. My husband would argue that I love sleep to a fault, commonly citing that if you sleep past 5:30 A.M. you have lost the morning. But I delight in the fact that if I wash my hair at night, lay out my clothes, and settle for a cup of coffee and some frozen item thrown in the toaster I can stretch the wake-up to 6:45 A.M. and still make it everywhere we need to be on time.

What I really love is when Saturday rolls around and my very understanding and loving husband allows me to sleep until eight. On those mornings, angels sing and trumpet sound because I am truly delighting in this extra hour and fifteen minutes. Chris knows it brings me joy and much-needed rest and has consistently afforded me this luxury since almost the first day we brought Ella home from the hospital. When I am able to fit in the extra hour, I truly feel rested. I wake without an alarm when my body is ready. I delight in sleep and am thankful that God created us with this idea in mind so that for a period of six to eight hours in the day we get to shut down and recharge.

When I am awake, **I love *Better Homes and Gardens* and *House Beautiful* magazines.** Really I love pictures of spaces and design that get my creative wheels spinning for anything I can replicate in my own house. I have decorated and redecorated each house several times and about fifty times more than that in my head. I can see a space and have it come alive with possibilities. Some day I dream of being featured in BH&G, but until then I'll settle for my latest copy while I curl up on my couch. Finding time to curl up with a magazine is a luxury that satisfies my creative nature. It's one of the talents God gifted me that I get to completely enjoy as a hobby. It's not my work to decorate my home or share advice with others; it's just soul satisfying.

I often save my latest issues to bring to the nail salon because **another great love is a good pedicure**. This is one of the tiny indulgences I have always prioritized, for a few reasons. We live in Florida, and eighty percent of my shoes are some variation of a flip-flop. No one wants to see nasty toes, so a fresh pedicure is practically a necessity. More than that, it's thirty minutes of quiet and pampering that is cheaper than therapy or a spa day and can pretty much fit into even the busiest of schedules. I partake in this every three or four weeks, so finding thirty minutes over the course of twenty-five days is typically something I can do without a great sacrifice. I don't lay out expectations for this in any given week, I just wait until the schedule lines up and there is empty space. I also don't buy into the idea that I deserve this indulgence because I work hard. I view this as a complete blessing, and each time I sit in that chair I throw up an arrow prayer of praise that I have the time and resources to treat myself in this way.

On some occasions I even splurge on my fingernails, but a fresh manicure doesn't last me very long because **I love using my hands to create something**, whether it's art, crafting, or photography. But this is one of those loves I've had to adjust because of this season of my life. I still make room for it, but it's usually with my kids. We will take out a giant roll of white craft paper and break out the Ikea watercolor pallet and dollar store brushes and get to work creating. In those moments when we slow down, sit together, and push pause on all of life moving around us at top speed, we find such sweet conversation and insight into each other's thoughts. With art supplies in the eight-dollar range, we have created beautiful masterpieces and memories of this time together. I may not be crafting in the traditional sense like I used to, but I can make a mean Play-Doh rose or pretzel, and my girls' giggles and creations bring me great joy.

I'm sure you're building your list by now. It might look like mine, or it might be something completely creative that I haven't even discovered yet. A few other loves are a good book, coffee, sitting on my front porch rocking chairs, swimming with my kids, snuggling with my dogs, date nights, home movie nights, our couples' life group, and my ladies' Bible study. God created me and knows me intimately. He is aware that these items draw me closer to Him because of my appreciation for these gifts. Your list of loves can morph and change, grow, or shrink as you pass through stages of life, the ages of your kids, your work life, and commitments. That's why it's important to make this list again and again. As you review what you have written down, I challenge you to change your thinking and shift your perspective. Believe that these items are not self-care that you deserve, but rather soul-care that you delight in when you have the time. Seeing these activities as blessings will create in you a sense of gratitude and praise, and there is never guilt in gratitude.

Chances are you can relate to falling victim to a lie that puts you above others. Even with our best efforts at blocking the enemy and guarding our souls, the lies have a way of entering through the cracks. Drawing near to the Lord and building a foundation in truth will give you the ability to recognize the lie before it penetrates your soul. In the long run it's going to make your life more full of happy moments, positive experiences, and a joy that is contagious to those around you. This type of joy fills your soul and reaches to the deepest part of who you are. It is joy that spills into your work, home, and relationships with other people, and it is contagious. That is a soul set on fire. You can still set goals for your career, seek advancement opportunities, and make time for yourself and the things you love, but you can do it with a soul-centered state of mind rather than self-centered.

Chapter 6 Application
Soul care 101

Your Body: If you now view caring for your body as an act of obedience and a commandment to preserve your temple, make a soul-care commitment today to form a daily habit.

- What is one thing you can implement each day to focus on your health? Write it because there is accountability in seeing your own words. If you need some inspiration, think of the following:
  - Drink half your body weight in ounces of water.
  - Eat out one less time this week.
  - Have meatless Mondays on which you load up on your veggies (this doesn't fly in our home, but a girl can dream!).
  - Take a twenty-minute family walk two nights a week.

Your Soul: God created us with unique talents and desires. He delights in seeing us live those out. Making space in our schedule for more of what we love requires we take an inventory of the things taking up space. As you work through the table, I challenge you to view it through a lens of gratitude rather than expectation. If this is a struggle for you, it's nothing that a little prayer can't accomplish.

Things that bring joy: *Example: Family walks in the neighborhood in the evening after work.*	Things I could give up to make time: *Example: Too many evening commitments that keep us from getting home before dark.*

Armed with your inventory of loves and time traps in hand, start to evaluate what you can do *today*, not tomorrow, to begin living for the things you love with an attitude focused on gratitude. And don't forget to leave room in the margins for beautiful interruptions.

Chapter 7

That Time I Was Fat:
Understanding You Cannot Have it All

Commit your actions to the Lord, and your plans will succeed.
Proverbs 16:3

Dear reader, I use the term "fat" loosely in this chapter. It's meant in jest, to give you a chuckle. I have enough understanding of the masterpiece God created me to be to reject the idea that a size 12 is fat or unlovable, so please do the same. Let's just agree that we will cool it, relax, laugh a little, and throw the word "fat" around like confetti. Because at the end of the celebration, you sweep up the confetti and toss it in the trash. That's where we will put the word "fat" and the idea that our weight, our pants size, or what the scale says has any bearing on how God sees us as His beautiful creation. So with that being said . . .

After having two babies, things don't go back to the way they were. For the healthy, fit, active mama, her return to pre-baby body is less of a struggle, but I can't exactly say I fit in that category. When my second little miracle baby was born I did all the usual back-to-pre-baby-weight activities of watching what I ate and being active so I could fasten the button on my non-maternity pants without needing a hair tie to extend the connection. I kept saying, "I have ten more pounds to go," for the better half of a decade, and what I actually meant was twenty pounds. I did all the things you're supposed to do, like pack your lunch with healthy options and bring your gym clothes to work with the best intention of making it there during lunch hour.

I was aware that my body was a temple, but during this particular season my temple couldn't pass the communal candy jar without taking a piece, or ten. I ate healthily most of the time and engaged in normal activity, but that was not going to be enough to drop the baby weight. I was not committed to a weight loss regimen, and this left me feeling like a failure still holding on to those ten pounds. The reality was, with two little ones at home I wanted to be done with my workday and home with them as quickly as possible. That meant working through lunch at my desk and skipping the gym because it would keep me from finishing what I needed to do that day. I'd get in the car and stare at that gym bag that had been packed for two weeks and start the self-destruction of guilt. One day I had enough of this feeling and just decided I was going to be fat. By fat I mean I was going to accept the ten (okay, twenty) extra pounds, dress to complement this new mom body, and find confidence in this skin until I was able and ready to really do something about it.

Despite the title, this isn't a chapter about weight loss. It's about the truth that you cannot "have it all." You will always be choosing what's important to you and prioritizing your time and resources to meet those priorities. At this particular phase in my life, I chose to be okay with ten pounds too many because what I would need to sacrifice to do something about it was not worth the gain (or loss in this case!).

In Chapter 6 we broke the chains of the self-care movement to embrace soul-care. By dismissing the belief that we deserve something, we can begin to shift our focus to serving others. As we discussed, this movement toward service does not mean we live without ever satisfying our own desires for fun and enjoyment. I think some of the greatest gifts God gave us are the gifts of laughter and enjoyment. There is no better nourishment for our souls than a good laugh or delighting in one of the desires of our hearts. You can live a life filled with faith, family, work, and servitude and still enjoy a great vacation or trip to the mall. You can have hobbies and interests and be a mom with a thriving career. But, and here is the big *but*, you may not be able to have it all and fulfill all of those desires *at the same time*. In this chapter we will look at those things you love and determine how they align with your professional goals. Laying the two side by side will allow you to prioritize what is of greatest value and determine which items may need to be put on hold at least for a season. Refusing to acknowledge the truth that you may have to make some sacrifices to achieve your goals can leave you in a pit of unfulfilled expectations, and I've never found joy in that pit.

I cyclically fall into the trap of believing that if I give up a little extra sleep and put on my superwoman cape I will be capable of satisfying this have-it-all mentality that so many working moms hold. But the road back to reality can be quick and painful. I have a real job with an actual boss and a team of employees that needs me on a constant basis. So many of the mom books of encouragement are written by incredible women who have become entrepreneurs and are running their own companies out of their home offices and answering only to their clients, readers, or subscribers. These women work hard and balance it all, but they are lacking one great big giant factor: a boss. Life looks different when you have accountability to an organization and a leader who doesn't necessarily share your idea of a work-life balance. Many working moms find they have a schedule packed with meetings and deadlines that doesn't account for a kid with the flu or the need for a day to just lay in bed and hit snooze about sixteen more times. Emails fly through the inbox at all hours of the evening, and some of them have deadlines that wouldn't be met if we didn't check email after work hours. As a society we have lost our perspective that the family comes first and become enslaved to all-access technology that we carry around in our pockets. I fight this new normal like salmon fights its way upstream, but there are just inevitable meetings or projects that derail my best intentions to put my family first. I have to leave room in the margins for the unexpected and then figure out how to balance all the rest.

This was what I was experiencing during that season when I chose to forgo the gym and accept my post-baby body. I wasn't unhealthy or risking my well being; I was just a little chunky and had to adjust to a tankini bathing suit with fuller coverage. My choice to give myself room to breathe and remove the pressure to look a certain way in exchange for more of what I loved was the best decision I ever made. That season of balancing the demands of my work with a new baby at home left very little room for anything outside of those two things. As my kids have gotten older and more independent, I've found time to reintroduce exercise into my routine, but when I can't get to it because there's a volleyball game or swim lessons after school, I resist the urge to feel slighted and just roll with the changes.

There are other things I gave up throughout the years. Some I was able to weave back in, and some I decided were not ever worth the time. In 2012 the biggest decision I made to give myself the gift of time was giving up Facebook. I used to spend hours a day checking my feed, reading status updates, posting photos, and leaving the obligatory comments on friends' posts. I would argue that this wasn't wasting time because I would do this in my "resting hours" at the end of the day when the kids were in bed. But the reality was, it was keeping me from doing anything else I really enjoyed with that time. We can become zombies who sit and scroll down our feeds until we look up and two hours have passed. Our culture would have us believe that if we disconnect from Facebook we are blocking our avenue to socialization and being "in the know." Social media has become our lifeline.

I'm not going to lie, I panicked a little at the first thought of disconnecting. But what I realized is that every time I went on Facebook, I wasn't left with encouragement or joy or feelings of contentment. Instead, I felt inadequate or like I didn't measure up, or I felt heated, like a red-hot poker, because people treat the social app as their platform to change the world one condescending, hate-filled comment at a time. When I came to the realization that this activity brought me very little joy and a whole lot of negativity, I decided it was time to give it a rest. Despite this realization, the idea of total detachment left me in a cold sweat, so I committed to a short-term fast. Could I really survive without this link to all of my high school acquaintances and long-lost family members several branches out on the tree? The FOMO—the fear of missing out, that if you're not connected and updated by the minute you'll be the only one left floating on a raft of isolation in the middle of the ocean—is real.

The fast was a short-term commitment to give up that activity and replace it with something good and godly. When I'd reach for my phone for a status update, I'd divert to a Bible app and read a verse. The result was this thirty-day commitment turned into six years, and the day I officially hit Disable Account, I didn't die. In fact, it was liberating to know that I don't need to know what you ate for lunch and see ten pictures of it to feel connected with you. I call more and text more and make room for people I really care about and can do life with rather than keeping tabs on the prom queen and secretly (and repentantly) delighting in the fact that she, too, has a couple extra pounds to shed.

Facebook may not be your crutch, and I'm not condemning it or saying it's a sin. Plenty of amazing Christians have even built their ministries using this app. At the heart of the matter, you know what your Facebook-like thing is. What is keeping you from fully living and enjoying time that could be redirected to other things? Hopefully you identified some of these things in the prior table and can pray over them and fast from those that are eating up your time. This isn't a free pass to never again empty the dishwasher. It's evaluating the choices we make to fill our schedules with commitments we should have been honest and said no to or entertainment that is bringing us down. When you do this, you make room for life to happen, to live in the present, and to experience the moment. Your life, this one you are living right now, wherever you are reading this, is so much more precious than any portrayal of life you are observing on Facebook. Get up right now and live yours! Make space to fill your cup with things that overflow it with joy, and it will start to bleed over into other areas of your life.

While it may be easy to disable your Facebook account or decline one of your after-school activities, we don't always have the luxury of saying no to the things in our professional lives that take up space. As an employee in a company with a corporate ladder, structure, and accountability, saying no to the things you don't like just isn't an option. I don't think you can apply the same principal of prioritization to the workplace when it means telling your boss you don't want to go to a meeting or stay late for an event that is part of your job. However, you do get to control the path your career takes and the steps along the way. Track with me a moment as I completely contradict the messages you hear from the world and ask you to evaluate your work.

Do you love your job? Do you feel you are exactly where God wants you, living a full and complete life with a balance between your work and your personal? Do you know your career path one year, three years, and five years out, and are you on pace to get there? If so, then fabulous! Stop reading this chapter, pat yourself on the back, and move on. If you answered no to any of those questions, I've got an exercise for you.

Working mama, what is it you are hoping to accomplish by getting up each day and going into your job? Are you punching a clock for a paycheck to pay the bills? Are you hoping to move up your corporate ladder? Do you strive for a $10,000 raise? I challenge you to get extremely specific in your dreaming. I challenge you to dig deep and know what it is you want out of this job, this career. Otherwise I'd argue that showing up each day, doing what you're doing now is going to lead you down a path that is the opposite of joy. Whichever path you decide you are on, OWN IT! In all caps! Bear in mind that you cannot have it all and check that the sacrifices you are making are worth the reward.

For years I spent my time focused on a title and salary goal. In my organization there are three primary layers of leadership: manager, director, and vice president. For the first five years, my sight was set on becoming a manager. I did everything I could do to prove myself worthy of that title. I asked for it and was turned down but listened to all of the specific reasons why I fell short of that promotion. I went back to work and focused on the shortcomings so that I would have tangible evidence of growth. A year later, I returned to my boss and asked for that promotion again but this time had all of the supporting arguments. My vice president was in a position where she could not turn down my request because I met all of the requirements to get there.

My expectations and plan were realistic. I didn't *expect* this overnight. Instead, I allowed three years to work my way toward achieving this goal. The next step of my vision plan was to become a director with a six-figure salary. I would come in early, stay late, attend after-hours events, respond to emails during evenings and weekends, and push my team and myself. I volunteered for every special project and never declined a request from my boss. The hard work paid off when my efforts were noticed and the promotion was granted.

With ten years of tenure, I moved up the ranks four times and tripled my salary. By thirty-three years old, I was one of less than 100 directors at our 7,000-employee organization, also among the youngest, and I had reached my salary goal. How did I get there? I made a detailed plan for what I wanted my career path to look like, and then I completely maxed out my plan ... by thirty-three. So it was at thirty-three I started with the "Then what?" questions. Sure, I could have focused on the next title and worked my way to it with the same force and overtime I had for the last two positions, but something changed when I peaked this soon. I didn't know what I wanted next and had established myself as a person who was in early, stayed late, volunteered for the tough stuff, finished assignments early, and barely came up for air.

Each promotion, each raise, each compliment, each time I was delegated something I probably shouldn't have been, I felt proud and accomplished with a momentary sense of joy. It was fleeting, though, because the praises of man quickly wear off and you find yourself on a slippery slope of working toward the next acknowledgement and chasing that next quick fix. At no point was I able to just sit back and relish in the accomplishments of my hard work because the past hard work was determining how high the new bar was set.

I spent two years reacting to the directives of my superiors with no real plan for my future. I accepted that if I set my sights on VP, there would be a lot at stake. My young kids, who already had such limited amounts of my time, would take a significant cut. My husband, who was working hard on his own career path, would have to step up his home game even more to fill in the deficit left by my choices. We would have to increase hours with babysitters and add on before- and after-school care. All of this would be worth the effort if this goal came with confirmation that this was God's will for my life. But there was a part of me that knew at my core this wasn't it. I realized I could not go backwards and undo the effort I'd put in, but I could make a choice about what I wanted the next thirty-three years to look like. I could shift my focus and perspective and find value in my work as it stood.

I could look for opportunities to grow and feel challenged without sacrificing the late nights and early mornings to work. Or I could decide that I wanted to pursue that next promotion and push pause on everything else to get there. There was no way to have both.

When I peaked at thirty-three and maxed out my plan, I asked myself this question that I want to ask you as well: Where do you want to be in one year, three years, and five years? Everyone has a pretty easy time with the one-year question, and most people have thought into the near future. It's the five-year question that often trips us up. I was leadership mentoring a fellow working mama in my organization, and when she mapped out her five-year plan, I asked her if she was willing and ready to make the sacrifices in her home life to get there. She stared back at me with a conflicting facial expression and finally replied, "I never realized that had to be a choice." Well, ladies, I would be bald-faced lying to you if I told you it didn't. If you just move full steam ahead and let your boss or employer continue to make that choice for you, you will eventually wake up and wonder how you got there. If you didn't have time to plan for the sacrifices and make adjustments to allow for them, the cost can feel far more painful and the reward less fulfilling.

Working mamas can embrace freedom to aim high and have big career goals. It is 100% okay to know what you want. It is also acceptable to tell your boss who offers you a shiny new promotion, "Thank you very much, and I am honored, but this is not the right move for me at this time," especially if you can say those words after spending time in prayer and consideration of God's best for your life. I know this because I did it on more than one occasion.

Six months ago, a new boss came on the scene. She asked if I wanted to take on a role she considered to be a privilege and a promotion. In addition to what I knew this role would take up of my time and energy, I also knew the work was not fulfilling and rewarding to me. Instead of reluctantly accepting it, I spoke of my talents and my ability to continue to deliver in the job I was doing and I passed on that opportunity. I didn't get fired or demoted, and I didn't lose her respect. Instead, that day I believe she began to understand who I was. I took a risk and verbalized that at this stage of my life, the ability to have work-life balance and flexibility in my schedule was of greater value than a title or promotion. I reiterated my dedication to my current role and assured her that I was content and fulfilled to continue on that road. She respected my transparency and awareness of my goals. I did not regret that decision for a single day. She continued to seek me out and offer me opportunities that were more in line with the desires I had expressed, and the results were lasting joy rather than a fleeting satisfaction.

You do not have to chase what the world desires for you. It is natural for our Spirit-filled bodies to desire more than worldly success or monetary gain. That does not mean achieving those is sinful. In fact, if that next step for you is VP or CEO or the top of your food chain, **that is so awesome**, and I pray God takes you there on a path that is rewarding. There is no shame or sin in chasing the dream, in achieving the top position or status, or in making those necessary sacrifices to better your family, if that is where the Spirit leads. Because the reality is, to be CEO or SVP at the top of the game, it takes really hard work and God directing your path.

This is the choice my husband has made with the support of our family. He works long hours and dedicates his time and attention to being the very best he can be at his job. He sells with integrity and honesty, and because of that, God has blessed him beyond what we could have envisioned. The rapid advancement of his career path allowed me to realize that we cannot both be on this path at the same time. It is not possible or fair with two little girls dependent on us. There was a time and a season when he stepped back in full support of my career and picked up all the pieces so I could climb. Now is my time to pause on my ladder and let him soar because I know the demands of our home life and the complexities of our work situations that are unique to us. I know we cannot have it all, at least not at the same time.

Only you can assess your family dynamic and determine the path you hope your career takes in the future. The best way to start is by mapping out what you dream it looks like while understanding God holds the pen that writes your story. Bear in mind that while it is important to think about your future plan, there is danger in allowing all of your own planning to get in the way of God's best for your life. I have lived in seasons when I felt my plan was completely in line with His and others when I could feel I was pushing and pulling my way through like a game of tug of war. I encourage you to map it out because this will prevent you from showing up to work each day uncertain of where you go from there. Then carefully pray over your map so that God can reveal to you areas where He has unexpected turns and tweaks.

Whether you can identify with the desire to be director by thirty-three and CEO by fifty or you are content to punch the clock and check your work baggage at the door, my prayer for you is that you know who you are in Christ. I hope that you can identify who you want to be and understand the sacrifices it takes along the road to getting there.

If you've never created a vision plan for your life that considers the personal and the professional, here are a couple of questions to get you started. Work through this exercise and then fold it into your prayer life. Ask God to show you how this lines up with His plan for your life and to enlighten the path to get you there. If your current situation requires you to embrace your fat pants, accept that sacrifice in pursuit of what really sets your soul on fire!

Chapter 7 Application

The vision plan

Professional Goal	One Year	Three Years	Five Years
Job Title			
Salary			
Employer			
Professional Development			

What are my three greatest professional strengths?
1.
2.
3.

What are my three areas of greatest opportunity (room for improvement)?
1.
2.
3.

In an effort to achieve my professional goals, I will commit to three things this year to set me on the path (examples: read a leadership book, attend professional development, find a leadership mentor, further your education, or have a discussion with your supervisor):

1.

2.

3.

Personal Goals	One Year	Three Years	Five Years
Faith			
Marriage			
Family			
Health			

In order to start a path toward accomplishing my personal goals, I will pick three practical things I can do to make room for those goals and chart the course to achieving them (examples: join a church, write a blog, join a gym or weight loss program, or read a parenting book):

1.

2.

3.

How well do your professional goals align with your personal goals?

In order to accomplish your professional and personal goals, what might you have to be willing to give up, pause, or put off for this season?

When you put the plan into words, it comes alive. It helps you determine what matters to you and gives you direction to pray specifically for the route it will take to get there. You may be surprised to see how far this plan can take you or how much you are willing to be ten pounds too many!

Chapter 8

Like a Boss: Transforming Your Approach

Lazy people irritate their employers, like vinegar
to the teeth or smoke in the eyes,
Proverbs 10:26

I've had several jobs in my lifetime, first in high school, then in college, and then I entered the real job scene. My first "grown-up" one came with a commute that made me contemplate driving off a bridge every day, not to mention the actual job was horrific. I sat in front of a computer and sorted spreadsheets with keywords for paid search engine advertisements. In any given moment I had to know the cost of over 10,000 different words for fifteen different advertising campaigns. I may have stretched the truth a tiny bit in my job interview regarding my access database skills, so I also spent most of my afternoons reading the *Access for Dummies* book I kept hidden on my lap under my desk. I wish I were joking.

Within the first few weeks of this first real job, it became abundantly clear to me that they call it "work" for a reason. I also realized that cubicles and I were going to have a very short relationship. At four months into my position, I was back on the job hunt in my spare time. On my lunch breaks I would go to a friend's house to use her Wi-Fi and send out applications by the hundreds. This first job taught me a few things: I didn't like Excel, I didn't like having a cubicle in a sea of other employees where we could hear each other breathe, and it does not pay to exaggerate a skill on your resume. But in this first job, once I finally got into meetings, presented some of my work, and got feedback, I came alive. I began to see my God-given talent unfold. I was the least important person in the room by far, but I could command attention, share my findings, and stand up to the questions.

Despite this new positive aspect to my job, there was a series of events with my first boss that began what I call my "walking-out phase." I spent the next two years job-hopping and walking out when the going got tough. I blamed all of this on each of my bosses, but the truth was, entitlement, immaturity, lack of awareness, and selfishness were all taking root in me. As I was adjusting to the working world, as much as I loved the idea of a job, the work itself was so much harder than anticipated. You move from college with classes three days a week, summer breaks, and long holiday breaks to a nine to five or nine to seven with maybe two weeks of paid vacation if you're lucky, and life as you know seems actually over.

If I had been better prepared for this harsh reality, I might not have been so quick to walk out (three times) and might have just realized that no matter who you are, what you studied, or what you're doing (unless you are the founder of Facebook in your dorm room), you've got to start somewhere, and usually it's at the bottom. Our work started at 9:00, and by 8:55 I already hated the day and hadn't even stepped on the elevator yet. This feeling was 80% attitude and 20% the actual work.

I wanted you to know that I have had bad jobs, made poor decisions at those jobs, and, most importantly, learned from those mistakes. I took those lessons with me and still reflect on them years later. I tell you about my job history so you can understand that it took a lot of hard work, planning and a few mistakes to get to the dream job. I'm hopeful that wherever you are on your career path, you can relate with at least one step of mine.

What's your current state? Do you feel a bit like you've settled or necessity pushed you into a place that seems impossible to escape from? I think it's important to remind you that what we are talking about here is actually *work*. It's never going to be easy, and if you are doing it well you're probably exhausted when it's over each day.

There are certainly seasons when even your dream job can feel more like a repetitive nightmare. So I'm not asking about a season of ups and downs. I'm asking you to look back on your last three months, six months, or even year and consider, can you find more good days than bad days? Can you say that you are fulfilling a purpose, making something beautiful, helping someone, or serving a purpose with the talents and skills God has gifted you? If not, keep on reading because chances are your boss is part of the problem, and we are going to tackle that with a solution.

We've all taken jobs just to pay the bills at some point in our lives, but my prayer for you and for me is that we can get to a place where even in those jobs the joy of the Lord is our strength. We can replace the face of our supervisor with that of Jesus and work as if it's unto Him. What does that look like? It looks like giving your all, being punctual, remaining thorough in your work, being a good steward of your time, and not taking advantage of your job. In my second job, I allowed my circumstances to stomp out my joy. I allowed my attitude at work and home to be infected by my job so much that it robbed me of any blessing that could be found in the work. My customers could see I was not enthusiastic, my coworkers avoided me because they knew I'd just complain, and my boss did not respond to my behavior by being more pleasant or lowering his expectations, quite the opposite.

Your job is your mission field. It may not feel like the Amazon or Africa, but it is the place where you spend thirty-three percent of your day if you work eight hours. The people you work with and God puts in your path are your mission, and your attitude is your testimony. We all know the person we hate to ask how they are doing because the response is always "Not so good," "I've been better," or a long tale of the latest negative thing that happened to them, because heaven forbid they are ever the one in control of their own joy. That person was me, and I beg and implore you, don't let it be you! You are so much more than a bad day, a horrible boss, or a bad job. You are a child of God, created in His image for His glory. Glorify the Lord with your work even if it's not where you want to be. And if you think there is something different for you out there, pray! Go to your heavenly Father and ask. His Word says so clearly to ask and you shall receive.

Jesus gives us permission to do this in Matthew chapter 7, where He is speaking to His followers and encouraging them to ask for what they seek. He wasn't handing the disciples a golden ticket to all they wanted out of life or permission to demand for all their wants and needs. Instead, He was teaching His disciples about the benefit of bold faith. He knows our future, and His will is best, but He wants relationship with us. Part of truly knowing Him is letting Him know all of us, including our deepest desires.

In my time of job turmoil and need, I prayed fervently for God to bring me a new job, a very specific job I had wanted since college. I know that you too can pray for God to change your circumstance, change your boss, open a new door, or just change your heart. Your request may not be delivered in rapid fire, or at all. Maybe you pray for a new job and instead He keeps you planted right where He has you now for the next thirty-three years. This may feel a bit like He failed you because He didn't answer your specific request. But what if the answer comes by way of peace throughout those thirty-three years? Maybe the best plan for your life is that you be defined by so much more than the title on your badge, the cubicle you sit in, the floors you mop, or the food you prepare. What if that job you are in is the setting for you to be a witness of the testimony of Jesus and there are people there who do not know God?

I don't know your future any better than I know my own, but I know I have prayed to be moved from a job or given a new boss or delivered from a fire and the answer wasn't immediate. Sometimes God calls you to wait, but it is in the waiting where we can see His greatness magnified.

For eleven months and twenty days (who's counting?!), I prayed for my dream job. When I learned there was a job that actually paid you to go out and talk to people in person, build relationships that would lead to new business, and network with people and bring them together, my mind was blown! I first encountered this position when I did a rotation internship with that organization my junior year of college. I spent four weeks shadowing this department and knew instantly this job was the dream. I have the gift of gab. It's a skill I developed as a toddler—I would tell random strangers about Jesus, talk my way out of any mischief I landed in (and it was a lot!), and carry on full conversations with my dolls with such robust imagination my mom began to worry if there was actually someone else in the room. I felt as if I had prepared for this job my entire life, and I remember leaving that internship and wondering if I could ever have a shot at it.

After several rounds of interviews, I had more than a shot! I got the job and it came with all the benefits and perks I was anticipating. The first few years at this job felt like I had won the lottery. I was on an incredible team, and the work seemed like it couldn't get any better. However, the reality of life is that even the dream job can start to feel like work, especially when you cross the threshold of becoming a working mama. Pre-kids, the nights and long days on the road were no big deal. But after having Ella, things changed. I wanted to be home earlier, and those thirteen-hour days felt like thirty. I was on autopilot, just going through the motions. In the early days of motherhood, figuring out this balancing act was front and center.

I eventually achieved some balance, and I did the dream job well. I found my groove and worked the only way I knew how, not as to man rather as if God were the boss. He was the one who could see me when no one else was watching. But the reality was, I didn't own my own business so I did, in fact, work for the man (well, it was a woman at first), and I worked a *lot*. One third of your life is spent in work. Read that number one more time so it sets in—one third. And that's if you know how to shut it off at the forty-hour mark. If that number isn't staggering enough, digest this five-digit whopper: 97,760 hours of your life will be spent at your job.

At about year five in my dream job, it started to feel a little less like a dream and more like *Groundhog Day*. I began to compartmentalize my life into these buckets that didn't mix or spill over. There was work Katie, church Katie, Bible study Katie, mommy Katie, wife Katie—I think you get the idea. I showed up in each version as if I were playing a very specific role. I didn't talk about parenting at work, and I didn't bring my faith into my job because I worked in a secular environment and I'd been told by the world not to bring discussions on faith and politics into the workplace. Life was tough having to remember which version of myself to be in each setting because the world had told me that faith was a weakness and I was working and living in that world.

Separating faith from my work made it easy to slack at my job. When my work wasn't appreciated by the people I was serving, I'd take an extra twenty minutes for lunch because no one was watching, or I'd spend an extra thirty minutes browsing the internet instead of pouring over reports. After all, I told myself, they wouldn't notice and I was underpaid and undervalued anyway, because twenty-seven-year-old Katie thought she knew pretty much everything about life. My career wasn't advancing, my daily tasks had become routine and boring, and my boss wasn't pushing for me to be any more than I was because she didn't know what I was capable of. To be honest, I didn't either. Only God did.

This autopilot stage went on for about ten months. I pulled into work with an attitude that was about as bland as a piece of melba toast, and I approached what lay ahead with so little excitement that finding a pulse in my work life was nearly impossible. My soul was longing for some salt and pepper. I sought that flavor by diving headfirst into being a mom and doing the whole self-care thing. I made my own baby food and scrapbooked with all the little stickers and embellishments, led a women's Bible study and read about thirty different books I'd been meaning to get to, binge-watched TV shows on the DVR and left early for play dates or other kid activities. I thought I was just prioritizing my family and my hobbies over my work, and many would even say that was the right way to live.

But Ephesians 6:6–8 told me something different: "Try to please them all the time, not just when they are watching you. As slaves of Christ, do the will of God with all your heart. Work with enthusiasm, as though you were working for the Lord rather than for people. Remember that the Lord will reward each one of us for the good we do, whether we are slaves or free." Because the Spirit was within me, the half-hearted way I was approaching my work was not sitting well with my soul. As restful as my new way of life should have been, it made me incredibly restless.

When Ella was nearing a year old, the guilt of being self-serving was heavy and the reward was light, so I decided it was time to make a change. The easiest path that came to mind was to dust off my resume and pursue other options that might bring a new challenge or opportunity. After my walking-out phase, you can see here that I had at least matured slightly. I kept my feet grounded in my current work while I prayed through what God's next step for my work life would be.

There was one very promising interview that had me contemplating leaving for the first time since I had landed my dream job, and this reality shocked me. I took some time in the stillness of the Father to determine if this was a door opening. There is nothing more conflicting or confusing than being faced with an offer that meets all of your desires, expectations, and requirements for a job but still doesn't seem like the reward you were hoping to unwrap. I prayed through this time of uncertainty, and the biggest comfort I found was in the promise that our God is not a God of confusion. In subsequent years, I would learn many times to find familiar comfort in this promise. So this time, I did not run, I did not flee; I stayed and I prayed.

In my staying, I realized that God doesn't divide the secular and the spiritual worlds. He wants it all to be spiritual. There are no buckets, just a free-flowing stream that can bubble over with such beauty into all crevices, caves, and paths of life. My path was not to find new work; it was to take the work I had and make it a God thing. I could no longer settle for the occasional victory of a compliment from my boss or little win of seeing my goals met in my job, so I set out to be different from my peers. I looked for a new path of success while redefining the way I accomplished my goals. I pushed myself to new limits. I listened with intent in meetings. I asked my boss what I needed to do to advance to the next level and followed every last detail. This was not all butterflies and smiles, though. It was tough. In that first conversation with my boss, she believed I should have been appreciative for the job I had and not asking for more. She verbalized this in words that cut my pride and gave me a heaping pile of humility. The experience also showed me I wasn't asking the right questions. I needed to stop asking her for a promotion and instead ask her to guide me in professional growth that served no other purpose than to help me learn, feel challenged, and grow. My job became about the kingdom. It became about serving the Lord rather than man and doing it all whether or not someone was watching.

This new approach should have left me feeling drained with

very little left to give to my home, family, and church. But it was the opposite. It is like when you make the difficult decision to tithe of your money. It seems like a Grand Canyon–size leap of faith and a mighty sacrifice, but as you step out one toe length at a time, God builds the bridge faster than you can walk. He creates the path farther than you can see ahead and blesses the gift beyond your measure. He did that with this new work life. The extra effort came easily and naturally as only He could provide. The colorful fruit that bloomed as a result was a new level of satisfaction in my work and my home. I even received a promotion in the process. Rewinding to the year before, when I was bored and believed the lie that I was getting less than I deserved, it is so clear why the Lord wouldn't allow me to taste that reward at the time. I had not earned it, and the lesson to get there was far sweeter than the instant gratification that would have come from being given something I had not worked for.

If you think you are in a dead-end job, that there is no future outside of the menial tasks you are faced with day after day, I would urge you to step out of that fog and make a decision. Decide to approach these menial tasks with new eyes. View your work as the Promised Land, a land entrusted to you by God. Or, decide to move on. It's as easy as that. Because if moving on is in God's will for your life, He will open the door, He will create opportunities you didn't know existed, and He will move you. If you don't believe it, just ask the mountains. He moved them without any trouble.

Aside from my own internal struggles and immaturity, the common denominator in the dissatisfaction with all of my jobs was my relationships with my bosses. All personalities aside, the only thing standing in your way of professional development, a promotion, a raise, or recognition is your boss. They determine the steps of your professional future and have power over your position, whether or not that's a fair or exciting way to look at it. In some select and unique situations, you can circumvent your boss on your path to success, but chances are, if you stay within your same company and grow in your current role, growth will always come from your direct supervisor. Whether you like them, hate them, respect them, or pray every day they will leave never to return, they are your roadblocks. Even if you find a way to leapfrog them, there will always be another boss waiting for you unless you jump to president and CEO. You will likely go through life in a job where you are accountable to someone on some level, and because of that, you have three choices when it comes to dealing with your boss:

1. **Stay** where you are and hope they quit, get fired, or retire (I am not advocating for hoping bad things to happen to your boss!).
2. **Win them over!** You might not like them any more than you did at the start, but you can work hard to prove your value and advance your career.
3. **Leave.** There is no shame in this decision if it is birthed out of prayerful consideration. It is better to get out and move on than to live in misery that is outside of God's will. But this third option will be so much sweeter if you try number two first.

The most miserable time clock punchers I know live in option one. They trade in their joy for a mediocre paycheck and stay at the exact same employment level for as long as they remain in that company, not because they are content, but because they feel entitled. They feel like their boss, their company, and their coworkers all owe them something, and they don't want to take a minute to have some accountability for their situation. Option number one is not for the person who loves their job and sees no reason to change it. It's for the Eeyore who walks around with their own personal rain cloud and sometimes leans over far enough to bring their little dark cloud into the paradise of others. I think true joy can be found in option number two, and that is where I'm going to spend my time here, teaching you how to win your boss over.

For many years, I spent my career in strategic planning and business development. The principles I applied to the strategy and implementation of a plan for my company to succeed are the same tools you can apply to your work life. I didn't realize this until we went through a series of leadership changes in my organization and I found myself on my fourth boss in three years. I wanted growth, recognition, and promotions with very specific raises, and the only way to get them was to follow a plan I had created many times before that began with considering my target audience. So let's focus on your direct supervisor as your target and build your plan to win over your boss.

Chapter 8 Application
Building your plan

1. THE VISION:

A typical strategic plan follows a formula that begins with a vision. You listed out the building blocks for your vision in Chapter 7. Based on those answers, what is your value and proposition? What is your big vision and goal? This is where you dream big and lay out what you hope to accomplish. You already defined where you want to be in one year, three years, and five years at your job. Hopefully you got very specific and gave yourself a title and monetary goal. You also looked at your personal life and the balance it will take to be realistic with your vision. Don't put "Become CEO" for your work vision if your personal plan says, "Have more family time and be class mom." Be realistic; make sure those two visions align because you cannot have one without the other. You most likely picked up this book because you are already a working mama or on your way to becoming one. Don't lose sight of your mom job, those responsibilities in which your true joy is found, when you consider your work vision.

Take a few minutes to define your own vision statement. This is one to three sentences that clearly state your goal for your role and responsibilities in your job today. If your vision is to not be in your current job, write that too.

Using the list you made for Chapter 7, write your vision statement below. Don't forget to weigh the personal sacrifices necessary to achieve this vision.

A vision is a big dream, an overarching idea and something to strive for so that you are not just showing up each day expecting something to happen to you. Your vision statement is for you. It's an internal belief and goal that drives everything else.

Now that you have your vision, determine how well your vision for your job aligns with the opportunities at your company. The way to understand which options exist for you and the road best taken to get there is by engaging your boss in the conversation. This is not just any conversation. It isn't a water cooler discussion or a stop and chat in their office when they are sidetracked and busy with their own assignments. This is a planned, strategic, and well-orchestrated conversation that will yield you all the answers you need.

I had three bosses over the course of four years, and with each one I sat down and had the same conversation. I started it with a series of questions that allowed me to do more listening and enabled my boss to define for me how I could achieve my goals. You may have had the same boss for twenty years and never probed or had a conversation like this. Don't let that hold you back. It is never too late to start. If you are intimidated by what your employer will think about your taking this initiative out of the blue, I can help you out there. As a boss myself, if one of my employees walked into my office and asked these questions, I would be thrilled to take the time to answer them. It shows resourcefulness and interest in growth. This conversation may be the very thing that puts you on their radar.

Obviously, every job and work environment is different, but you can guide your conversation with one or more of the following questions:

- What is the vision and mission for the company as a whole?
- Does the company or organization operate off of a strategic plan?

- What are the priorities for our department in helping to carry out that plan?
- How do you define success for our team?
- What goals are important to you as our leader?
- How do you measure our success as a department?
- How do you measure my individual success?

Do you notice more of these questions are about the organization and the department than about you personally? This is not an opportunity for you to ask for a promotion or what options are available for you. We haven't gotten there yet, and even though you may feel that the work you do day after day is enough for a promotion, there is a strong possibility you may just be doing the job they hired you for. Knowing the answers to these questions will help you understand your boss better. They will help you determine what is important to them and what clicks. Circle the questions that can apply to your conversation and use the space to write up a few of your own.

Strategic Questions:

_____

_____

_____

2. THE PLAN:

I made the mistake on two occasions of asking questions one and two and stopping there. One time my boss tossed me a fifty-page strategic plan that I would have needed a translator to interpret, and it didn't help me understand him or know my role any better. It was in these inquisition failures that I learned from my mistakes, went back, and changed the questions.

The single most important question you can ask of your boss is, "How do you define success for our team?" That question drives your plan and gives you a clear indication of what is most important. This doesn't mean you abandon all the other tasks associated with your job; it just means you *always* lead with that.

My job is a form of sales that consists of a long cycle of visiting a prospect before closing a deal. One of my bosses always defined our success in a qualitative way—how many visits did we make, what was the quality of those visits? All of this was documented in a very extensive report detailing each event and interaction. If the report was completed by the deadline and full of details, we had met our objective.

When I was faced with a new boss who had a different approach and possibly a strong case of undiagnosed ADHD, I handed him this sixty-page report and his response with wide eyes was, "What on earth is this?" I explained that this was the way we proved our value as a team, that he needed to read this report and understand our detailed interactions. He chuckled and told me that was never going to happen. He explained that he was a numbers and return on investment guy and that I needed to show him the dollars and cents. He wanted transactional sales. I had never been asked to do this before, and in order to figure out an effective way of meeting his request, I asked for permission to ditch the sixty-page detailed analysis that had been consuming my time in order to create a new way of reporting our progress. I dove in full force to figure out a report that met his specific needs. I did not have to guess what those needs were because he had already defined them when I asked the right questions.

No matter what line of work you are in, your job has an objective and your boss is either satisfied or dissatisfied by some level of activity. The activity itself can vary greatly from job to job. For most of my grandmother's career she made toys in a toy factory. Her goals were black-and-white and quantitative and could have been something like this: complete twenty-five tea sets per day. Asking her boss to define her goals would have probably yielded, "Complete 25 tea sets a day," with a tone that had some level of "Duh!" attached to it, but I still would have encouraged her to ask the question even if she thought she knew the answer. Maybe there would have been some other quality or safety metric she would not have paid attention to otherwise. This is why it is important for you to ask the questions particularly when you think you know the answer!

Equipped with the answer to the most important question, now we build your plan. Fill in the blank lines with the specific definition of what success is at your workplace. According to my direct supervisor, success is defined as:

_____

_____

_____

Now let's evaluate your current state. Where are you right now on the road to achieving this success? And what changes can you make to your work to make this a priority?

_____

_____

_____

3. THE MEASUREMENT:

Even the greatest plans are of no value without a means to measure the success. Think about a family vacation you plan. Let's say you spent weeks researching your family trip to Disney World. You plan the meals, character breakfasts, rides you must hit, shows you must see, and shops you can't miss. You have high expectations for this expensive vacation, and whether consciously or not, you will measure the success based on certain metrics. Those metrics may be quantitative, like checking off the number of rides you are able to enjoy, or qualitative, like observing the pure joy on your kids' faces after each ride or the smiles as they inhale one of those Mickey Mouse–shaped ice cream bars with chocolate dipped ears. Either way, you will assess the results and measure the success based on some type of reaction. This measurement will craft a response and summary of the trip, and you will either go home telling others you visited the happiest place on earth where all of your family vacation dreams came true, or you will write Disney a letter suggesting they change their brochure to show the reality of overtired kids, parents yelling, and nine-dollar lattes.

Your work plan is no different. You need a way to measure the success of the goal and the plan you set for your fulfillment and career advancement. If your boss said that their number one priority is seeing the numbers and knowing the return on investment for the service you provide, start a little portion of every day dedicated to that project.

As I mentioned, I didn't know anything about this at first, but I was confident there had to be someone out there who did. I tapped into resources like vendors, contacts at other organizations I had met at conferences, my former boss, and my employees, and I googled it. I found message boards and even used an online ROI calculator to plug in my numbers to see what it would do. Chances are someone before you has paved the way in your industry, and unless they are a direct competitor, they may be flattered and more than happy to share some resources. If you come up empty and have exhausted every avenue, go back to your boss and explain all the ways you tried to find the answer and ask for their guidance.

What metrics can you use to measure your growth and success? If there is no defined form of measurement, what resources could you engage to create metrics for measurement?

---

4. THE REPORT:

Once you have a means of measuring the success, take some time to collect the data. Our organization was heavily focused on the quarters of our fiscal year. I spent two of the four quarters implementing my new plan and measuring the success of our department with the metrics that were important to my boss. It took me several weeks to come up with a formula that would adequately show the hard work and dedication of my team in a revenue-generating measurement. Once I had this, I didn't run to his office with the number; I spent six months capturing this measurement and trending it. We did not always grow month over month, but that was not what he asked me to do. He asked me to show the measurement and prove our value to the organization in a dollar amount. I was able to deliver on this request and take it a step further by applying detailed explanations for the months when no growth occurred. They were not excuses; they were accounts of lost business due to factors outside of our control.

I compiled all of my findings into a brief PowerPoint deck that started with a slide that stated my vision: show a return on investment. I included the findings from our meetings on a discovery slide under the vision section and detailed the plan I had crafted based on the vision. I rounded out the brief deck with two slides that described how I came up with the metric of measurement that led into a couple of slides explaining the results from six months of applying this concept. In eight short slides, I had radically shifted my boss's opinion of who I was as an employee. This was not something he had asked me to do, but I was confident it was not a waste of my time because I had already asked the questions. I understood what was important to him and reported out on those results only.

What happened that day in his office was a pivotal moment in my career. He grabbed the report, told me to put on my suit jacket, and abruptly stood up and told me to follow him. I was practically jogging down the halls of our organization to keep pace with him. I had no idea where were headed. We rounded the corner by our main admissions area, and in a cold-sweat panic I figured out where we were going. He waltzed through the double door entry of our C-suite administration and brought me right into the CEO's office unannounced. I followed his lead and sat down in the chair adjacent to him, and he began the conversation in this way: "Did you know that we have this small department in the basement of this place operating in a way that generated us $12 million in new revenue last year?" I could hardly believe my ears. He was referencing the findings of my report and talking about my department, and he had never once even fact-checked the slides.

The slide presentation with my boss could have gone any number of ways. He could have questioned my findings, challenged my results, or dismissed me completely. I had mentally and emotionally prepared myself for any of those outcomes but certainly not for what actually unfolded. Because I had taken the time to ask what was important to him, listened, and applied changes to the way I worked, we were speaking the same language. I was not working exhaustively on a report that was sixty-five pages long that no one cared to read. I was able to shift my focus, time, and attention to the priorities that met his needs, and the result was a promotion two months later.

Your vision, your plan, and your measurement are of no value if you can't determine a way to report out what you have done. Maybe a PowerPoint presentation is intimidating to you. If so, handwrite your findings on a sheet of legal paper or type it in a Word document. If your goal seems a simple one, like Grandma making twenty-five tea sets, you should still write it down. And if you have six months' evidence of exceeding your goal, they need to see that in black and white. When you deliver your report, do it with the utmost humility. This is not about you and how great you are. You are great—we already know that because you are fearfully and wonderfully made—but pride and overconfidence are surefire ways to deter your employer from seeing your true value. Be strategic about the delivery. Schedule time when you will have their undivided attention, reference that first meeting when you asked them to define all of the goals, and clearly deliver the results.

I cannot promise this will get you a promotion or pay increase or that your boss will waltz you into your CEO's office. But I can promise that you will never be disappointed that you tried. There is freedom in knowing where you stand in your organization. If you follow the plan and it doesn't have a fruitful outcome, at least you know that you gave it your best. You didn't walk out or give up, and I'm sure you will learn something along the way. If you sit in the first phase of just waiting for something to change without doing anything about it, chances are it never will. You will be in the same job with the same boss and the same misery unless you learn to be in control of what it is doing for your soul.

Sometimes when we work for someone else, we feel we have little control over how our story plays out and what happens in our career. Because we don't own the company or make the decisions, we feel helpless. Instead of viewing it this way, I empower you to decide what kind of employee you want to be and accept whatever the result is from your decision. If you want to be noticed, given new challenges, and potentially promoted, take a look at your work style. Are you the first to arrive or the last? Do you stretch your lunch or put in extra minutes to finish your day? Is your work as flawless as you can make it? Do you work just as diligently on the projects you don't like as the ones you do? Do you greet others with a smile and carry with you an attitude of gratitude?

As a boss for many years, I can tell you this will make all the difference to yours whether you know it or not. I can see subtle differences in my employees' work ethic, and even though I may not comment on every action, I am committed to plucking those who went the extra mile out and creating new opportunities for them to grow.

This is you, taking some control over your job. You are deciding to work in the best way you know how, choosing to step up your work game to be noticed and stand out from the crowd. If applying these changes to your life doesn't have any effect because you just have one of "those" bosses, keep that resume fresh and explore your options. If you do start to be noticed and appreciated for going the extra mile and told that you are looking great and asked what's changed, stay humble. Remember whose you are, why you're here, and who is writing your story.

Chapter 9

Money Is Not A Dirty Word:
Money Myths and Matters of the Heart

For the love of money is the root of all kinds of evil. And some people, craving money, have wandered from the true faith and pierced themselves with many sorrows.
1 Timothy 6:10

Money is not the root of all evil; the Bible says the *love* of money is. Yet *money* is one of the few dirty words that isn't comprised of only four letters. We've been told that it's the thing you don't talk about. You don't share your salary around the office, you don't broadcast how much you paid for your house or car, and you rarely read about it in a book unless it's a financial one. And typically, Christians don't list it as one of their goals. They may think about it, like maybe you did when you were formulating your vision plan. We may think there is shame in making monetary goals because we have been conditioned to believe we just don't talk about money. We've already talked about aligning your personal and professional goals into a vision plan. Then we put that plan into action with the purpose of winning over your boss or dusting off the old resume and seeing what else is out there. It only seems fitting that we turn to a discussion about money now. Because at the end of the day, whether we love our job or not, we all go to it for the paycheck. We can be minimalists, we can be budgeters and cut back, but there is no avoiding that we need money on some level to live. So let's talk about money.

What are your beliefs around money? We have to start there because your beliefs will determine how you read and take in this chapter. Do you think Christians shouldn't talk about money? Do you think it's a dirty, sinful word? Do you fall into the category that believes if money is part of your vision plan you are somehow disappointing God, so you write the words but erase them?

Do you know when people actually start talking about money? When they run into money problems, they are short on their bills, the debt has piled up, or there is a deficit. Then people talk. They may broach the subject by asking for prayers, or it may come in the form of a plea and a request for help or an outpouring of complaints and comparisons about what they cannot afford that others have. Our churches are no different. Most pastors avoid the topic because they believe it is a turn-off, that it drives people out, or that it offends parishioners, all of which are partly true. But, when it's time to build a new building, fund a new ministry, support a missionary, or take a look at the red in the budget, the sermons on tithing and money start in full force.

If people talked about money more, there would be fewer money problems. I don't just mean talking about our bank accounts; I mean addressing the way we look at and treat money. For starters, it is not a dirty word. Do you know how I know we have the freedom to talk about money? Because the Bible talks about it somewhere between 110 and 120 different times, in both the Old and New Testaments.

The concept of currency and payment for debt has existed since the beginning of humanity. Adam and Eve weren't exchanging currency with each other for their fruit and fish, but the minute sin entered the world, so did debt. Someone or something had to cover the debt of their sin. Before sin, they had everything they needed to live, prosper, and eat. Once sin entered the world through their free will, God instructed they would have to exhaustively tend to the ground for what they ate, making their food a form of currency exchanged for their hard work.

You, working mama, go to work because you need the money. You've got a lifestyle, bills, debt, and financial goals that depend on it. We are no different than Eve; we are all just working hard for the money.

Don't you just love when we can relate to the very first humans and find comfort in knowing there is nothing new under the sun? Sure, we've got better fashion than fig leaves and far more to spend our currency on, but the idea of debt, payment, savings, tithing, and enjoying the gifts God has granted us is not new. God created money. So where does all the confusion come from about whether we should talk about it? How do we balance our goals and gains with being good stewards of what God has entrusted? I believe it begins with the heart.

When you think of the heart, what's the first thing that comes to mind? Probably not the scientific diagram of the living, beating organ (at least I hope not because that is not where this illustration is going). Chances are, you think of the Valentine's Day version, the red heart shape emoji that symbolizes love. Money is a heart issue because the Bible is so clear: you cannot love God and money. You can *like* money, you can appreciate money, you can set goals for money, you can spend money, you can save it, and you can give it away, but you should not *love* it.

The term *love* probably sounds a little cliché and easy to disregard because you are likely thinking, *I don't love money. I don't physically embrace it or curl up next to it at night. I don't fill my bathtub with dollar bills and do a pretend backstroke through it set to a soundtrack of rap music. So I must not love it, right?* But perhaps you do cringe a little when you see someone on the side of the road in need of a couple bucks or you do get heated when the pastor gets up and asks the congregation to give over more hard-earned money to the church that already has enough. Do you get fired up when you get a nail in your tire and it costs you an extra $250 that month that you didn't plan for? Or does it anger you when you forget to hit Pay on your online bill pay and you get a call from one of your lenders asking you why you are five days late? What right do they have to call you when you always pay on time?

Well, sister, they have every right. For as long as you have debt, you are enslaved to your debtors, and unless you were born into a trust fund of epic proportion, you are going to owe someone something for a portion of your life. The goal for you and for me is to someday experience financial freedom, but for some of us that may never be a reality. And that little twinge you get every time you are asked or forced to unexpectedly part with your money—that's the love we are talking about. What we can experience, starting today, is soul freedom from the bondage of guilt about money, and we can learn practical ways to unravel our love affair.

I am going to ask you the most overused question in the Christian church, one that either you are going to be quick to answer with a complete lie or you are going to get so aggravated with you might toss this book across the room. But if my questions didn't cause a stir in your soul, what good would they be? So brace yourself. Take at least ninety seconds to think about it before you actually answer, and don't be so literal. God isn't coming down from heaven and speaking by way of burning bush or sending you a DM. Here goes:

> *If God called you to give up all that you have to follow Him, would you do it?*

Allow me put it in terms you can relate to. If you got called into your boss's office tomorrow and they said, "Thank you very much for your years of service, but we are downsizing, and effective immediately, you are no longer employed," would you still follow Him? Would you trust Him with your future? Would you keep tithing, keep believing that He has a plan for you? Sure, you would stress out; we all would. Or you may cry and panic for a day or two. But at the heart of the matter, can you really trust Him with what is next?

Or say your church staff calls you into a meeting and says that God has pressed it on their hearts to ask you to lead a team moving to a remote country and live in missions. Would you at least pray about it? Would you check in with the Holy Spirit to see if this was a true calling on your life?

For many years I answered this question so wrong, and what I realized was that even without my bathtub filled with money and Run-DMC playing in the background, I loved money. I spent several years in bondage to money. I worried about our bills, our savings, our surplus, and our financial future. I took budgeting to a new micro level and was continuously stressed every single time I swiped my debit card. These feelings were not derived from some discipline to a God-ordained budget; they were fear because I loved my money and I didn't want to live without it. I did not realize that my love for money was the root of the anxiety, that it was what was destroying my joy in my earning, spending, and giving. The fundamental problem with this season of my life was not how much we made or how we financially planned. It was one tiny little three-letter word, *our*, and the belief that what we had been given actually belonged to us. It was not our money; it was God's.

Maybe that upsets you. Maybe you feel that you work really hard for your money and that because God doesn't deliver it on the backs of pigeons to your doorstep it's not from Him. That's okay. I didn't come to this understanding overnight. But I hope I've asked a question that stirs your soul and that causes you to question God on the topic or maybe even test Him.

This is actually the *only* topic on which God welcomes us freely to test Him. In Malachi 3:10, the Lord says, "Bring the full tithe into the storehouse, that there may be food in my house. And thereby put me to the test, says the Lord of hosts. If I will not open the windows of heaven for you and pour down for you a blessing until there is no more need." Right there in His Word, we are told to test Him. Bring the tithe, and He will open up the blessings. It's not for us to understand with our human mind why God needs the money when He has the power to rain it down from heaven. In fact, I'd argue this has nothing to do with His need and everything to do with you and me. He created us, so He knew fully that we would be prone to love money. He knew it would be that one thing in all of creation that has enough power over us to become an idol. What He is asking of us when He commands our tithes and offering is that we trust Him with it all.

If you read up a little further in Malachi chapter 3, God calls a lack of tithing "robbing God." The only reason to use this language is that God views what we have as His. And before you get all hot and bothered about His taking possession of your things, think about the fact that He is the one who breathes life into our lungs and He only asks us (very specifically) for ten percent of our money. He lets you and me keep ninety percent and then promises to bless and stretch that ninety percent. I don't know about you, but that's a lot more than I can say for the government, which takes upwards of thirty percent of my money, and I don't argue with them on whether or not they've earned it or if it belongs to them. If you want soul freedom from the burden of loving your money, you've got to be willing to give up the first ten percent.

This is not easy, though, when you already love money, when you haven't been tithing, when it doesn't fit into your budget, when you have other debts, or when you can barely make it from month to month. Maybe you are in the red, borrowing more to piece it all together, and this seems like an impossible and guilt-inducing commandment. You may feel guilty because you now know you should have been doing this all along and it's just one more thing you can't afford. My family has been there. When God first began to work on our hearts as a young married couple, we already had a stack of bills and very little surplus. We threw in $100 a month when the plate passed at church, but it was out of our surplus, not our first earnings as the Bible commands. In those early days as a married couple, in order for us to be tithing as the Bible commanded, ten percent would have been $440 a month. That felt like an impossible stretch in our budget, a number we just couldn't part with because we had prioritized all of our other debts ahead of this. When we only gave God one fourth of what He commanded; how could we be surprised when He only returned one fourth of the blessing?

When we were struggling with the topic of tithing, we used arguments like, "Our pastor drives nice cars and lives in a better house than us; they don't need our money." If that is your holdup, your crutch for tithing, here's what I recommend: First, pray over it. Pray that God changes your heart on the issue and reveals to you the ways your tithe would be advancing the kingdom. If you still can't get there because there is no evidence of wise spending in your church or there is extravagance in your pastor and his family's lifestyle that does not seem in line with the budget of the church, find a new church. We let this particular argument keep us from tithing for far too many years. We saw a pastor and his entire family employed by their independent, non-denominational church. They lived in extravagant homes, took five-star trips, and lived lavishly. Shame on our money-loving souls for expecting our pastor to live in poverty or have no investments, but nevertheless, we caved to this temptation to judge. Our misconstrued ideas of their financial situation only festered because the church had no governing board or accountability to keep them in check. We finally resolved that if we could not give freely and joyously in this church, we needed to find a new one where we could.

When we give to God, we shouldn't be focused on where it goes, but we also should be holding our churches accountable to be practicing the same stewardship with their money that the Bible commands of us individuals. This does not mean that the church scrutinizes the personal spending and investments of its pastoral staff; rather, it applies what the congregation gives in a way that serves the church and paves a path to reduced debt. If your church won't share its balance sheet, what its budget is, and how it is pacing, that would be a great place for you to start to ask the questions. Unfortunately, there are churches in the news every day that misuse funds given to them, but even if you were victim of a church where that happened, try not to get hung up on that. Focus on the fact that your giving is the result of a command and not every church behaves this way.

In our tithing debate we also rationalized our lack of a full commitment by telling ourselves we should be credit card debt–free before we tithed. We kept using those credit cards and increasing the balances, all the while arguing, "But we have to." We are not the budgeting type. We will never have a detailed ledger sheet of all the money coming and going, we rarely put limits on our weekly or monthly spending, and we are conditioned to go out and buy what we want. So at the time we had a general idea of what we could spend each month, but we did not get down to the penny. If we wanted a big purchase that we didn't quite have the money on hand for, we would buy it on a credit card and plan to pay it off with a bonus check, Christmas cash, or the sale of something else it would replace. The possibility of hitting credit card debt freedom felt bleak when we had no actual plan in place to get there. So this created a safety blanket for us, what we believed was a valid excuse to God for why we didn't tithe, and we pinky swore we would get there soon.

My husband and I also didn't exactly agree on the topic of tithing. I grew up in a home where our family gave to our church regularly. Chris grew up Catholic, and the topic wasn't even emphasized at his church. When we married, I felt it was something we should be doing, but we were not on the same page—he didn't agree that tithing was necessary. For a few years I nagged him, until someone shared with me that God would not want dissension in our marriage over this, or any other topic. If I was going to submit the authority over the financial state of our household to my husband, I needed to submit all of it. I stopped nagging, and I prayed, quietly and fervently, for two very specific things: one, that we could both commit to coming out from under our credit card debt, and two, that we would share the same desire for tithing.

In full disclosure, I was equally as quick to spend the money we had and the money we didn't. And Chris was always very generous. Any time he saw a need from another person or a cause he was moved by, we gave. We just lacked that ten percent commitment to our church. We bought into the lies that everyone uses credit cards, everyone carries some debt, ten percent was a lot of money, and we were no different than anyone else.

What it actually took for us to come to the decision to tithe was finding a new church where the pastor really talked about money. Not the church's need for us to open our wallets to help them meet their budget—this was a mega church with a several million–dollar budget, so they didn't *need* our money. They were in a position where they used their surplus to find new ministries and missions to support. This pastor talked about the relationship to money itself, what it does to us if we let it become our lover, and how hoarding it contradicts God's best for us and places us in bondage, and he very unapologetically shared the commandment in Malachi 3:8. What this man wanted to do was release his congregation from the bondage of money; he wasn't trying to build the church's bank account.

The hard-hitting truth spoken about our love affair with money started to change something in our family. We realized there was freedom in not owing to credit card companies and that not everyone has credit card debt, so we did a very difficult thing. We cut them up.

We kept one card in each of our wallets as an emergency backup, and it was the one with the lowest balance.

I knew several people who had come to financial freedom through Dave Ramsey studies, so I began to do some independent research on it. While his principles and steps are foolproof, they take incredible restraint and dedication and neither of us was ready to go that distance. However, I did find one tip I thought we could apply, and it slowly made a difference. Ramsey calls it the "snowball method" of paying off your credit cards. At the time we had about four or five cards with balances ranging from $800–$4,000. Monthly, we were paying $150–$200 on each card and seeing very little impact in the balances while feeling every bit of the nearly $1,000 a month coming out of our bank account. The snowball effect says to stop doing it this way and instead start with your lowest balance and pay the most on that card. Pay your monthly minimums on all the others. This let us pay off that one with the $800 balance in less than two months. It was liberating and addicting to be able to open the invoice each month and see a zero balance. Then we moved our way down the list. This process required no change in our budget, no sacrifice in our spending; it was just a shift in the way we paid. We also opened one additional card that had a 0% APR offer and transferred our highest balance to that card, knowing that would be the last one we got around to paying off because of the snowball.

Seeing the debt lessen and shutting down one credit card account after another changed how we wanted to spend. We were increasingly more excited to see the balances go away and no longer making purchases on them. For three years we watched card after card disappear until our only debt remaining outside of our house and two cars was $5,000 in credit card debt and $5,000 remaining on a student loan. In that third year we received an unexpected inheritance of exactly $10,000. We stood with that check in hand and could have made a number of decisions with it: go on an awesome vacation, buy so many of the things we had passed up, fill up that bathtub and try the backstroke, put it in our savings account, or pay off our debts. We chose to no longer be prisoners to our credit cards and loans. The feeling that came after was better than any purchase or vacation would have been. We both felt that the number was so specific that we couldn't see any way not to use it to cover the debt. What God was doing with that gift was freeing us to be able to give of our surplus, prepare for emergencies, and have freedom to buy and do the things we had once only dreamed of.

It was somewhere along this journey of ridding ourselves of the debt that Chris took a huge leap of faith, without any probing from me, and wrote his first tithe check. It was before we had a surplus, when money was still stretched thin, but God had done something in his heart to relinquish the love and possession of the money we had been entrusted. He consciously handed it back over to Him. I had prayed for many years for this to happen, but God had His own timing in mind. That single decision to hand over what was not ours was a pivotal point in our financial circumstances.

God blessed the remaining ninety percent again and again and again. And with that blessing we have been able to meet the needs of so many others. What we have is not ours. We earmark certain portions for our future, emergencies, kids, comfort, and fun, but when God moves in our lives to present us with a need, we now have the financial freedom to help meet it. It is a thrill like no other and a humbling reminder of where it came from. We also learned to only be loosely tied to our plans for our money. If we get that unexpected flat tire and it takes $250 out of our account, this is an opportunity to praise God that the money was there to cover it.

We have grand ideas of retiring on Lake Oconee in Georgia some day and contribute to retirement accounts set up for our future, but our plans are written in pencil, with God holding the eraser. Larry Burkett points out in his book *Jesus On Money* that the concept of retirement is not actually biblical, despite our preoccupation with it. You won't find it anywhere in the Bible. It's not to say retirement is a sin; we just have to remember to leave room in our plan for God to reroute the course of our life, if that is His best.

I've already established that my family is not mega rich. We went through seasons of financial ups and downs and ran the race of buying whatever we wanted even when we couldn't afford it. At this point, you might have formed a strong opinion of me. You might think we made huge sacrifices and did something extreme. Perhaps you are picturing us as two folks in homemade clothing, growing our own food and never eating out or vacationing in order to become debt-free. That makes sense. I get how it might appear this way, and that is probably exactly what I would be thinking if I were in your shoes reading all of this in a book. So this is the point in the story where I need to bring some reality into this discussion.

Chris and I still have a mortgage, and while we have plans to pay that off faster than the terms of the loan, it will still take us several years because this past year we built our dream home complete with the quartz countertops, subway tile backsplash, and hardwood floors. I also have a single pair of shoes that cost $700. Although it is slightly embarrassing to admit that, we have got to be real here, and there is just something about a pair of red-bottom Christian Louboutins that makes me feel like I have just stepped off of a runway. We just got back from a vacation to Hawaii. It was our fifteen-year anniversary, and we planned, saved, and paid for it all a year in advance. We flew first class in those special seats that convert to beds and stayed in a cottage that was featured in a movie. We lease new cars and change them out quite frequently. We have a weekly date night with a standing babysitter and sometimes go out to a fancy restaurant just because.

Why on earth am I telling you all of this? It's not so that you will envy my lifestyle or compare yours to mine or to promise you that if you tithe tomorrow someone will send you a pair of Louboutins (Although anything is possible! Why should we put limits on what God can do?). I am telling you this so you can see that I am human and do not live in a bubble or earmark every dollar I earn for saving and tithing. When I follow the commands of God's Word to not let money control me, to hand over the first fruits of my labor through tithing, and to reduce my debts, I feel the freedom to enjoy little indulgences that the surplus provides us. I know exactly where that surplus comes from, and I am so thankful to Him who provides it. I am not enslaved to the goods or vacations; I am incredibly and overwhelmingly appreciative of them, which is exactly what I believe God desires.

Some people think I should feel guilty for owning a pair of $700 shoes. They think that *because* people don't talk about money. It's not that I make so much that $700 on shoes is a typical Tuesday purchase, quite the opposite. They were a present and something I had dreamed about having for more than a decade after I saw Angelina Jolie wear a similar pair of black patent leather pumps just like these on the red carpet to an event. Chris purchased these shoes for me after we'd paid our debt, tithed to our church, given of our surplus, and saved for some of the things we had dreamed of for several years. Choosing not to buy me those shoes wouldn't have made a difference for those things we prioritize; we would have easily spent that money in a series of unnecessary trips to Target or on cash wrap items at the grocery store (because we weren't using Shipt yet!). Besides, it all goes back to the heart. I do love those shoes, but I love God more. And if He called me to give up the shoes to follow Him, I might shed a tear because I'm human and they are so beautiful, but so be it. He is so much more valuable than well-crafted, patent leather, red-bottomed shoes.

God calls us to seek Him first, to seek His kingdom above all else, but in that same command He gives the promise, "Seek the Kingdom of God above all else, and live righteously, and he will give you everything you need" (Matthew 6:33). There are countless warnings to the rich about how difficult it is to love God and money, but there is also promise after promise that He will provide for our needs, He will reward hard work, He will entrust the faithful with much, those who are diligent will reap a harvest, and if we abide in Him and ask, all will be given to us. He is not an angry God on the seat of judgment looking down at this earth and pointing His finger at all of those who do not choose to live in poverty for poverty's sake. If He has entrusted you with much, praise Him for it, thank Him for it, and be willing to give it all up and follow Him, if that is the calling.

Now that we have established that what money we have is actually God's, let's talk about bringing God into the planning. I don't think we should put limits on what God can do once we admit to ourselves that He will provide, especially in the area of money. Three years ago, our church set a very lofty goal—one that was money-focused. Our pastor stood on the stage in front of our congregation and proclaimed that we had outgrown our humble building and that the lack of chairs and rooms for kids was putting limits on how many people we could reach for Christ. He said we needed a new building, but he was more than confident that God was calling him to lead our church to do it debt-free. The dream was to raise a very large amount—three million dollars—in a short time of only three years. It was a big dollar figure, so money was certainly part of the plan, but God was too. Our church staff and board could have decided to take out a loan, which would have been a perfectly acceptable thing to do to build a new space. But faith was bigger, and they believed God could do it. It is now three years later and less than one week away from moving into that new building, and because of 652 families who gave faithfully, we are entering it with zero debt. Out of 4,000 churches that our contracted financial firm works with, we are the *only* one to have achieved this. Why? Because our leadership, our pastor, and our congregation were not afraid to set a monetary goal. Perhaps a three million–dollar goal seems extravagant, but God helped us accomplish it because it was for His glory.

As a working mom, your personal finances are no different. If you invite God into the planning, He can help you achieve financial freedom, He can bless your surplus, He can allow your dream home to become a reality, or He can bless your finances enough to give you the freedom to walk away from your job. Whatever your financial state, however much you make or want to make at your job, inviting Him into the planning is a great place to start. Because this is not just a book for the super wealthy executive moms with $700 shoes. We also need to address the reality that perhaps you've got a money problem. Sister, feel no shame, I have been there.

There have been seasons in our life when money was tight and others when money was flowing. In all seasons, however, our hope was still found in the Lord, and while paying bills was easier when we had extra money, we were happy and grounded in all of them. During one of those seasons of being stretched tight, we had just settled into being new parents and the overwhelming expenses that come with children. Ella was eight months old, and we felt a sense of financial pressure that we needed to be released from. During that time, I prayed for God to use skills he had given me to start generating additional income—web design and photography. Ella was sleeping so much in the evening, and I found extra time when I gave up Facebook, so I spent that time dabbling in these skills, took a leap of faith, and offered to take on some clients. I grew a small business of family photography, professional headshots, and websites for other small businesses just like mine. This wasn't a desire to get rich; it was just an avenue to build up the surplus to supply some of our needs and wants without having to go to the credit cards. At first it was slow and steady, a couple hundred dollars a month, but God grew that into a great supplemental income for that season. The last wedding I photographed earned me a $2,100 profit. For three years it helped me to meet a specific financial need and recognize talents that would serve me well for many years in my career.

Maybe you don't have a camera or never took Photography 101 in college like I did (I just needed the credits to graduate), but I promise you that you have at least one marketable skill. The internet is bustling with sites to help parlay whatever your skill is into a business. For starters, you're a mama. You've got the marketable skill of caretaking, which means you could put an advertisement on Care.com to bring another kid into your home a couple of hours a night or whenever works for you. You could sign up to be a Shipt shopper and take on a couple of other families' grocery lists while you shop for your own. There are also countless ways you can build and grow a home-based multi-level marketing business. A friend I met on this book journey has done incredible things with that, and she's written her own book about becoming a balanced entrepreneur. If you have the desire and a little extra time, this may be a route for you as well. My only caution in entering into a business venture is to be sure the initial investment is not going to put financial strain on you. Some of these opportunities have limited risk, and there are countless people who have gone before you whom you can tap into for direction.

Okay, I can feel your eye roll; and hear your cynical thoughts: *Yeah right, now you want me to get another job? Didn't we already establish I'm a working mom with not enough time as it is?* If that sounds like you, if exploring options for additional income just does not seem like a possibility in your current situation or maybe you already have the second job or small business and things are still tight, you can always look at your expenses. One of the biggest expenses for a working mama is childcare. In fact, this is one of the big factors most women take into consideration when deciding whether or not they will go back to work after having a baby. Through prayer, and lots of it, God delivered on this in my life in such a big way that I feel I would be cheating you of your cover price if I didn't share what I learned here.

In Tampa, the going rate of traditional childcare is between $160 and $280 per child for a week of full-time daycare. If you would prefer a nanny without a DUI or prison record, you are looking at $17–$30 an hour. When I was making my decision about going back to work, all of these options seemed so far out of reach and did nothing to help the money anxiety. So, I did what I do when there's nowhere else to turn: I prayed.

God revealed His plan and blessed us with the absolute greatest caretaker we could have asked for outside of immediate family. Susan, you are a blessing. Meadow has spent every week in Susan's home since she was five months old, and she is now four years old. This is our last year with Susan full time, and I get misty-eyed just thinking about that. The truth is, when Meadow arrived, staying home wasn't an option with our existing lifestyle, and Susan gave me the peace of knowing that someone was stepping in as my substitute. You, working mama, need a Susan! And if you need to know how to find her, well, sorry, she is all tied up this year, but be resourceful. I posted a very specific advertisement on Care.com and described every one of my requirements (think Jane and Michael Banks in Mary Poppins). Within two days I had nineteen applicants, and the minute I read hers I knew she was the one. I didn't follow some miracle formula, nor do I live in the best town for nannies. It was because I prayed and did some research. I learned that the cost was a fraction if you looked for someone willing to open their home. On average, you would pay $30–$40 per day, and in my situation, I only needed three days a week. Every daycare I looked into was going to charge me for full-time, whether I needed it or not. Finding Susan, who met my specific requirements, allowed my girls to spend one day a week with their grandma and one day with me. If you do your background check, conduct a home visit, check references, and trust your gut, you may just find your Susan. Over the years she has become so much more than our childcare. She is part of my village, she cares about our entire family, and she is special to Meadow.

Finding suitable childcare for your babies is the hardest step in returning to work, and there are so many anxieties that come with it. Who will watch my kids? Can I afford it? Will they be good enough? And like everything else, I tried to control it to the point of obsession until I realized I couldn't and turned it over to the Lord. He knew the plan even before there was a plus sign on the pregnancy test, and His way was best. If finding the perfect caretaker and being able to afford it are top of mind, I urge you to pray.

If childcare is one of the biggest expenses on your home ledger sheet, consider this: Do you have your kids in a prestigious daycare because you have bought into their marketing scheme and some fancy sign on the door that contains the word *academy*? When you see that word associated with infants and toddlers, you might be fooled into believing the caretakers are conducting military-style training or teaching advanced physics beyond those doors. Whether you call it an academy or "Tender Loving Care," your baby is crawling around on the floor, putting anything they can grab in their mouth, and hopefully being lovingly embraced and rocked to sleep. There are so many years of their life when the school you pick matters, but in the early years, what matters is love, affection, and gentle instruction. You want safety, security, and the assurance your child is getting the best substitute for you, which doesn't have to come at the highest price tag. Just apply your prayer and some research, and this may be one area where you can make an adjustment.

The last prayerful step you can take today to change your financial situation is to look at your job and your salary. When I asked the question about the way a Christian should consider money in their goals, I was leading you to see that God should be invited into all parts of our lives, including the money part. When you develop your vision, plan for your job, and goals for your career, it would be neglectful not to consider money (unless you are in full-time volunteer service). I very specifically set a six-figure goal for my income in my vision plan. That goal was not driven by a materialistic motivation; it went hand in hand with the type of job, scope of work, and title I was seeking. I knew at a minimum that was the salary a position like that commanded. Defining the financial aspect of my career goal was about knowing the value of my work. It was not about filling the bathtub with dollar bills or stacking the closet shelves with countless boxes of those fancy shoes. It was the value I put on the sacrifice of my time. There were distinct times throughout my career when not being in touch with the value of my time would have cost me greatly.

After a number of organizational changes and restructuring, I was asked to take on two other departments after their leadership was eliminated. I initially accepted this challenge with no expectation of monetary gain because it was supposed to be temporary and I was a team player with zero experience in either category. When the temporary gig seemed to have no end in sight and the workload had tripled, I knew enough about my value to ask for a salary increase. I brought the facts—the total amount saved by the elimination of two other full-time employees along with my new list of responsibilities— and called attention to the fact that I had received no additional compensation. My boss was not upset; he was actually surprised to hear that this was overlooked in the shuffle of leadership changes. That single conversation is what pushed me across that six-figure line and helped me reach my goal. I got there because I knew the value of my work and prayed over the discussions.

God could very well call my family to poverty. We could lose our jobs, lose our house to fire, have to give up everything with which we have been entrusted, and face the true test of where our hearts really stand on money. We could be called to sell it all, pick up our nets, and follow Him, just like He commanded the disciples. You and I can invite Him to pull up a chair at the table as we fill in our vision plans, we can consult Him on the salary goal, we can tithe, we can give out of the first ten percent, and still He may have something different for us then what we write on our plans. Can we trust that He knows best?

Chris and I have come a long way in our financial plan. We spend out of our abundance and indulge in many of our desires. We plan and save for our kids' college funds and our retirement accounts, and we have an emergency fund. But we also know that all of the dollars that make up those funds, all of the things we have purchased with that currency, is just on loan from the one who provided it all. We don't love it, we don't serve it, we don't allow it to lord over us, even though the temptation is strong at times. And we don't make any of those choices by our own strength. It's all because we listened when our pastor started to talk about our relationship with money. It's because we choose to bring God into the planning and openly discuss money in our home. It's because we understand that regardless of having the greatest financial planner or the fattest retirement accounts, God can still change the plan. He can reroute the course. He can call us to poverty or allow financial misfortunes. And even still, He will provide our every need and there can be joy, unspeakable joy. So I urge and encourage you to start today, talk about money!

Chapter 9 Application
Money talks

If you are blessed to have a spouse, you and your husband need to talk about money. If you're a single mama doing this alone, find a friend or trusted advisor you can use as a sounding board. Regardless of your marital status, you need to start the conversation. Wherever you are on the path of your financial plan, there is no time like the present to start making plans and goals for your money. Before you begin the conversation, listen very closely here: You do not need to nag or blame or point fingers about which one of you got you in whatever situation you are in. The topic is already stressful enough, so set the tone by de-stressing the environment. Don't let you kids interrupt you seventeen times to open their juice boxes or get them another snack. Go out to your favorite coffee shop or wait until they are sound asleep and brew your best blend. Pull out two chairs at your table, silence your phones, and bring your Bible and a pen and blank paper. Here is where you begin:

- **Invite God into the discussion.** If you and your husband don't regularly read the Bible together or pray, no big deal. We don't either. But when there is something at stake, something important to discuss, we know that God needs to be present, and there is no better way to invite Him into the third chair at your table than by welcoming His word.
  - Open up to Malachi. One of you read chapter 3, verses 6–15.

○ Pray. If this is awkward and you don't have the words, one of you just read the following:

Lord, this is weird for us. You know that. But we want to try something new. We've been doing it our own way, and we want to invite You into the conversation about our money. Soften our hearts. Put us on the same team. Create in us a love for You that is so much greater than that of money. Thank You for all that You have blessed us with, and help us to find a pathway to freedom from debt and the fullness of the blessing of tithing to You.

○ Now start talking. Where are you today? What are the major stressors? Take that blank sheet of paper and jot down three things that put strain on your money. This could be your three biggest expenses, unforeseen bills, your salary, influx in commissions, taxes, etc. Maybe the two of you don't share the same three. This is why you need to talk.

○ How can you practically tackle just one of those stressors? Highlight the one you agree would be the easiest to tackle. Remember the snowball concept? Don't worry about your biggest problem; start with the easiest. Which one can you start today to make a change to or have an impact on?

▪ Are these expense or income problems? Are your expenses too high and you need to figure out a way to lower them? When you are on the same page about what you are tackling, you may be able to find new ways to reduce the expenses.

▪ Or are there no further cuts you can make and the only option is increased income? Talk about ways you can add to this. Can one of you use one of those very marketable gifts God has granted you to pick up some extra income? Are there things you can sell? Never underestimate the power of resale. Nextdoor is a great app to sell things lying around your house that you are not even using. One day on a standard playroom clean up, I made $160 just by posting things I would have otherwise taken to Goodwill. There are people out there who will just about buy anything!

o   What is your biggest barrier to tithing the ten percent God commands? If this is an area you just do not agree on, don't feel convicted to do it. Or if you are struggling with the concept of what is really God's, just talk with each other. Talk about it in a loving way, an understanding way. Find out where you each are on the topic and write it down. Why? Because in six months or sixteen years when God moves in your heart or changes your feeling on this, you want written proof to reflect on how great He is!

o   Check in with your salary. Know the value of the work you are doing and how it lines up with your compensation.

  ▪   Glassdoor.com is a great place to get an idea of what others in your industry are making. Talking to your own HR department about how they assess your position for market and cost of living changes is also enlightening.

  ▪   If you are finding discrepancies in your pay, lay out a scope of work. There are hundreds of examples on the Internet you can follow, but you can start basic. List the primary tasks you are doing and write out what they entail. Line that up with your job description and highlight the areas where you job has grown or changed since you started. Pray over what to do with this information once you have it. Maybe you have a conversation with your boss or you start to look for other job opportunities more in line with your pay.

o   Spend some money. When you go to the extreme, cut back on every frivolous item, reduce your Starbucks runs, or say you will never eat out again, you are only setting yourself up for failure and robbing yourself of the blessing of enjoying what God has given you. Spend some money; there is freedom in Christ to do that. And take the opportunity to profusely thank Him for the ability to do so.

- Decide as a couple which of your frivolous spending options is important to you. In our home we prioritize our date night. We pay a babysitter one night a week so we can have a night out. If we run into a tight month, I will cut back on Target trips and Dunkin Donuts coffee runs, sacrifice buying the organic milk and getting a pedicure, but we will not cancel our sitter. We need that night of three or four hours to connect and recharge our relationship so we are better prepared to tackle all the messy stuff as a united front.

- Set a big goal. If you are going to tackle paying off a loan or a credit card or building your surplus, what is something big you desire to do with your first surplus? Maybe it's a dinner at a new posh restaurant in town, or a new outfit for each of you, or those fancy red-bottomed shoes. Don't be disappointed when that goal takes longer to reach than you might have planned; just put some fun into all the stress of talking about money. For years Chris and I dreamed of going to Italy. We talked about how that would be our "one day" trip. We had a very traumatic house flood situation in our early married years that basically tore our house apart completely, but out of the floodwater came an unexpected blessing of a $2,800 surplus because of cost cutting and doing some of the repairs ourselves. We took that $2,800 and went to Italy because we knew what our big goal was. We didn't have kids yet, our debts were minimal, and it just seemed like the right time to celebrate after a season of upset.

o Allow the blank paper to guide you to whatever else you need to decide about money. Maybe you need a micro budget. It annoyed Chris to no end, but for a season we needed that. Maybe you need to try a Financial Peace University class by Dave Ramsey. Maybe you want to consult a financial planner to make sure you are making the most of what you have. Maybe you give each other a high five and walk away from the table with a little spring in your step because you nailed this money thing. You get to decide here, and no matter what you decide, yay for having the conversation!

o Schedule a follow-up conversation in six months to see how you're doing and keep the talk going. Money is not a dirty word, and if you get to a point where you layer those dollar bills in your garden tub, pop some bubbly, and dive in, you owe it to yourself and the rest of the world to snap a pic and tag me, @fortheworkingmama!

If you are looking to break into the multi-level marketing business or at least hear more about it, send an email to katie@fortheworkingmama.com and I'll provide you a list of my personal friends who have seen success in active wear, beauty products, and health and fitness. Some of their companies even have dual benefits like making extra money while getting yourself in rocking' shape.

Whether you have too many expenses, not enough money, or perhaps find yourself sitting pretty, the key point to remember is whose money it is in the first place. While it may be difficult for our human minds to comprehend surrendering all that we have to someone we cannot see, His Word is clear and His promises are abundant to bless those who chose to faithfully submit in the area of their finances.

Chapter 10

Let's Get Real: Parting Words

For I know the plans I have for you, says the Lord. They are plans for good and not for disaster, to give you a future and a hope.
Jeremiah 29:11

We've reached the final chapter before we part ways. To this point you've hung in there and listened to me talk about parenting while growing a career with a plan and purpose. We have chipped away at the lies the world feeds us about how we should work, and we have (hopefully) gotten in touch with our souls. Living with a soul on fire doesn't come overnight; it takes time and effort to keep the flame blazing. But my hope is you have discovered the right tools to make it happen. Now you may be wondering, what is the big finish? I hope this doesn't disappoint you, but this last chapter is where I strip away the advice and the lessons and get real with you about my current season as a working mama.

This is the hardest chapter for me to write, because I am right in the midst of a season that is challenging and at times seems impossible to persevere. If I have misled you on this journey with the idea that I have it all together, then you have read it all wrong. Many of the truths that I have learned came out of my own mistakes, challenges, and sometimes sins. I am a human who can do brokenness just like the best of them. I didn't set out to write this book to tell the world how perfect I am but rather to help others through my story. My goal was to save a few people from the same mistakes, to be vulnerable, and to let God speak to my own life through the words He would give me.

With that buildup, here is my truth: I do not have it all together. I do not know all of the answers. I don't always accept what God is telling me. And sometimes I still sit in my closet and cry real crocodile tears. There are times when I allow my thoughts to become so negative that my reactions are rife with sin. At the present time, I feel like someone has folded up my body, stuffed it into an Instant Pot, and turned it on pressure mode. I am trying so hard to be perfect—to work perfectly, wife perfectly, parent perfectly, and not bleed any added pressure or stress onto my husband, who has enough of his own. I do most of this alone because I am terrible at asking for help. I don't want to inconvenience others. I will often find myself at my wits end and then yelling at my husband or my kids because they didn't see I needed help. This is a crazy way to live. I know it, and yet I step back into it every morning. Our life has sped up to a pace I can't recognize with meetings, activities, travel, and so many different demands on our time.

We use our village as much as we can to fill in the gaps, but there are just times when someone forgets to pick up the four-year-old from the sitter. When we become so busy, distracted, and torn in multiple directions I know the reality of who suffers. It is the two innocent little girls who are looking to their parents to craft a home that is their sanctuary and provides them security from this crazy world. The world tells you lies that are meant to make you feel better about pouring your whole life into work: "Your kids will look back on these days and won't even remember you weren't there," or even better, "Your kids would rather be playing with friends or with a babysitter than home with you." I've had both of these said to me on multiple occasions, and they do nothing to fix the guilt.

We know we can drop the guilt when we replace it with truth, and I've tried to point you to as many of those truths as I could cover throughout this journey. The trend of this story is that I typically don't just encounter lessons one time, master them, and move on. I tend to find myself in similar situations over and over again with new details but familiar challenges. I believe this is because as much as our hope can lie in knowing our God is not a God of confusion, we must also expect that our enemy is not creative. He knows where our cracks exist, and he comes back at them over and over again. If he tripped us up once, he will attack the same weakness, just like any other predator.

One of my favorite movies is the original *Jurassic Park*. There's a scene where the park security is explaining the raptors' intelligence to Dr. Grant. The confined predators keep attacking the same security fence in different spots to find a weakness. You can build up a security fence around the things in your soul that the enemy comes after, whether its your work, marriage, family, or finances, and our raptor enemy will keep coming back at that fence until he finds the weakness. It's important we face this reality. Because to tell you that we tackle something once and then it is settled forever—the vault is sealed, never to reopen—would do nothing to help you. We are not immune to these attacks; in fact, we are more susceptible when we are on a path to freedom and living for the kingdom.

I am thirteen years into my dream job, and I am standing in the same valley of confusion I visited earlier in my life, praying for discernment. I find myself at a crossroads where the dream job has morphed, twisted, and evolved to the extent that I am not sure I am living my dream. Maybe this is because I don't really have a dream at the moment.

I have allowed my work to adapt to new leadership, staff changes, and specific duty and role changes. If I am not in a season of change, I struggle to find a comfort zone. I continue to visit my vision and plan for my work, but for the past three years, my only constant has been change. Believe it or not, this book journey is an interactive experience. Every application I've included I selected with both you and myself in mind because I am not going to ask you to do something I'm not completing right alongside of you. The reality hit when I sat to write my vision and complete my plan. I cannot plan for three to five years from now, because when I look to the future, it is blank. I cannot even bring myself to write out my one-year plan for my work because when I look to tomorrow I have a sense of urgency to be anywhere but here.

I have had more job opportunities fall in my path in the last year than most people get in a decade. I have turned the same company down on three different occasions and still sit here today with another offer from them. I've expressed my concerns to my current employer, and they have met every one of my demands, yet I still find unrest. As anyone would hope, I have learned from my past mistakes, so I am not reverting back to the time I checked out, low pulse and no drive. But I find myself sitting in a waiting room, anticipating God's *next* for my life.

Everything I have achieved to date is exactly what the world tells me I should want. I am a leader in my organization with a staff, an assistant, and that six-figure salary I once only dreamed was possible. The reality of all of it, though, is that it mostly feels meaningless. I have brought the spiritual into my work, and I have become bolder in expressing my faith. There are no longer little buckets of Katie that never spill over. But I am still in a place of uncertainty. God continues to bless the work I produce and create opportunities to showcase that work, which makes this all the more baffling.

Last Sunday in our church service, our pastor delivered a sermon on King Solomon and his pursuit of happiness through everything under the sun. The man who had it all had nothing apart from God. He had achieved success and wealth to the highest degree and yet still found no fulfillment. We walked out of the service and my reaction to those words was: *I might be wasting my life in a job I am good at, that is safe, and has security but in essence is meaningless.*

The higher you climb on the corporate ladder, the more that is expected of you. In all of my envisioning and planning, I never wrote the words *become vice president.* This role would be at least a few years from a reality, but the one thing I've learned is you need to know where your career path is headed, and it is the natural progression from the role I hold today. If I want to advance beyond my current position, that is what lies ahead. When I sit and daydream I could get caught up in the fact that achieving that next step is a very attainable goal, but my reality is that step comes at a cost I am not sure I'm willing to pay.

In my workplace, achieving VP status comes with an enormous list of demands on your time outside of your day-to-day responsibilities. Not only do you carry the heavy weight of the role and all it entails, but you have signed on to be one of a small, elite group of people who represent the organization at every community event, public appearance, breakfast, luncheon, dinner meeting, and the like. You take administrative call on the weekend and round on staff as needed. Perhaps if I were a doctor called in to save lives, a scientist developing a cure for cancer, or a rocket scientist responsible for the safety of passengers on the way to the moon I might think differently, but in my line of work of sales and strategy, there are no emergencies, no life-altering outcomes. It's a completed deadline, executed project, and thorough report. That is not worth trading any more than I already have. While I often feel I don't know much about tomorrow with any certainty, I can confidently proclaim I do not want that life. Besides, making people refer to you as Mrs. Vice President probably gets old.

The Bible has a great deal to say about work and the role that men and women should play beginning with the first couple, Adam and Eve. Adam was created first in the image of God, with a purpose of working in the Garden of Eden. When Eve was brought on the scene she was given the role of "helper" to Adam. Many modern-day scholars try to argue that this principle was sexist and is culturally irrelevant. Whether or not we get into a debate about the significance of the submitting wife, the truth of God's purpose for husbands doesn't change. They were built for work. Adam was created for work before sin entered into the world. Work was not a consequence of sin but was an intended use of Adam's life. That same inclination for work is rooted in our men today. Throughout Scripture, references point to men bringing home the bacon because God has built them with a desire and need to provide for their families.

Maybe you made the decision as a couple that your husband would stay home and you would work. Maybe your skills are more marketable, your degree has more weight, or your opportunities are more lucrative. Whatever the reason, if that's you, please don't feel any judgment, just love. You know your situation best. You checked in with God along the way, and no one has a right to tell you what you're doing isn't His plan for your life. In fact, in my marriage there were many years when my W-2 was slightly higher.

For nearly a decade my husband dedicated his career to education. He began as a teacher and was on a pathway to administration. We made a decision together that he would pursue this passion, and while his path to financial "success" would be slower, the time he would have with our children would be invaluable. I would not trade the fact that he was able to spend his summers with our girls when they were young for any amount of money. We had an abundance of time together as a young family and still managed to live a very comfortable life. When Chris decided he felt God's calling on his life changing directions, I was selfishly hesitant and sad because I felt he was walking away from his talents and the gift of time his job afforded. But God used that transition to pull him out of a comfort zone and into a career he was made for.

When you think about the picture of someone who loves their work, works for the Lord, and as a result sees such overwhelming blessings, that is the man I am privileged to call my husband. I have seen both sides of the coin—the one where he took a less demanding role that put him in more of the caretaker position and the one I see him in now as the true provider. The change in his demeanor cannot be denied. God built him for provision, for strength, and for adversity. I could never handle his role the way he does. I would be so emotionally tied to every decision and so personally offended by every rejection that my commission check wouldn't be enough to buy an ice cream cone. But he does it, and he does it well. In our home there can't be two chiefs, and by chiefs I mean CEOs. Neither of us is there yet, but as I see that as a very plausible step in his future, I know that I cannot desire that for myself, at least not this side of a decade. We consciously brought our girls into this world with a desire to raise them to be strong, independent, hardworking, God-fearing women, but they won't get there by spending two thirds of their life with other people.

In Chapter 8 we discussed that we spend a third of our lives in a typical forty-hour-a-week job just by punching the clock. To sacrifice more time than that of my girls' precious childhoods is not worth the addition of a comma in our bank account or the highest title I can achieve. It all comes at a cost, and fortunately, I've already learned the hard way that you cannot have it all . . . that time I was fat.

The world tells you my thinking is crazy. They even have a term for this idea I am defying: "the power couple." The power couple works crazy hours, makes several hundred thousand dollars a year, has the kids in the finest private schools, and maintains a payroll of nannies. And here I argue that the power couple is just plain missing out. Would you like to talk about some real power couples, some examples I can get behind? Let's talk about Abraham, 100 years old, and Sarah, 90, getting busy and having a baby! Whoa! Or Noah and his wife, Naamah. The man builds a boat in the middle of the desert, flocks animals in pairs, and tells his wife to climb on board. These couples heeded very big callings God placed on their lives, and they were not missing out because the world said ninety-year-olds couldn't get pregnant and it had never rained before. This is the type of power couple I hope my husband and I will be—one that is on fire for the kingdom of heaven, one that furthers a purpose so much greater than just a job. My job can certainly be part of that story, but pouring in the extra hours to accomplish fleeting success just doesn't seem like my calling.

Can you see my dilemma of where I go from here? Can you relate? Or are you stuck thinking that your financial situation is so dire that neither of you will ever be VP or chief of anything but your own grief? Well, ladies, I believe that God placed this book on my heart for this very reason, and I am here to tell you that if you are a zebra who wants to change her stripes, the zebra needs to pray. Just four short years ago if someone had told me we would be where we are today I would have laughed in their face. We had just had Meadow, and something about the freshness of a new baby started to change me. I did not find myself rushing back to work to escape the newborn, and almost every day since I've had the thought in the back of my mind that maybe, just maybe, I am developing the new desire to be home or work in a less demanding field. I began to speak this to my intimate circle of Bible study babes, and they asked me what would have to happen to make that a reality. I said a miracle.

Teachers are not paid enough, and even with Chris's career track to administration it was going to be slow and steady. I saw no feasible way in my immediate or distant future that this tingling pain and seed of a desire could ever come to fruition because we had built a lifestyle upon on two incomes. Like with every other mountain in need of moving, my babes and I began to pray over it . . . for four years. We prayed God would align the desire of my heart with His will for my life, and we prayed that God would somehow, someway, take Chris's career and get him to a place where he would make just the equivalent of our combined income. Do you notice how specific the prayer was? I prayed for a dollar amount, because that was what my human brain could comprehend. I didn't pray for more, just what I thought would be enough to put a net in place so that if one day I needed to jump, there would be a place to land.

Today, four years later, God has just blown the roof off of my specific prayer and the limits I set on Him. I thought it a miracle for Him to double Chris's salary, and instead, no exaggeration, He has quadrupled it. I'm not promising you that if you rub the magic genie in a bottle all of your money stress will go away; I am just promising you that absolutely nothing is impossible for our God. If He had not chosen to answer this prayer in this way, I would have continued loving and trusting Him, because I said it myself, it would have to be a miracle.

God answered this prayer because He was rewarding Chris's guidance of our family and his financial decisions. As his earnings started to increase, he paid off our debt, and in his biggest leap of faith he started to tithe. I had prayed for almost eight years that he would tithe (and sometimes I nagged), but God had to work in His own timing to reach the heart. The sweetness of that answer to prayer was greater than any dollar amount that was deposited into our account. Chris didn't tithe out of abundance. He began when it was still a sacrifice and an unknown because he was putting God to the test to provide again and again. If you desire for God to change your financial situation, you have to make him Lord over it. Recognize that all we have is from Him and belongs to Him anyway. And if you and your spouse don't share this conviction, just pray! It may take eight years or forty-eight, but I guarantee you will learn some patience along the way.

God has answered the prayers I set out for the past several years, and He has even delivered on those I didn't pray. He worked in my career as I handed it over to Him and brought the spiritual into the secular. He blessed our family and our finances and has made it feasible that one day I could take that leap and try something new with my time or stay home. He has opened doors and closed doors and allowed me to walk through times of uncertainty just so I could find Him and cling to Him for stability. He has done all of this to show me that regardless of my job title or job satisfaction, it can be well with my soul.

And here we are full circle; I am back in a season of uncertainty. I have two back-up plans. I have a job offer from another company and a possibility that I could walk away from it all and stay home. I am struggling every day to find joy in my current job knowing that other options exist, but I have no confirmation from God that either of those is the answer yet.

The steam started breaking free of the pressure cooker I've been stuck in this past weekend. I internalize my feelings and stress to a point that they eventually have nowhere to go but out, and this time they blew up in the direction of my husband, initiating a pretty good fight. A small situation that could have been defused was escalated because the pressure had me. In our nearly fifteen years of marriage with ups and downs, a season of counseling, and a whole lot of work, we have learned to fight better. The ugly part only lasts a few minutes before one of us throws up the white flag and says, "Let's talk about this." And talk we did, for hours. We are both under stress, we are both coming up short at home because we are stretched so thin, and I am feeling my needs aren't being met but can't articulate what those are.

Lately, every time we come back to this type of discussion it brings us to the topic of my job. I find myself believing that life would be so much easier if I didn't work because I could just fully manage the house and he could fully manage the work. But we both have so many fears around that idea. I fear that I will not know who I am outside of work. It has been part of me for my entire adult life. He fears that he will be under that much more pressure to be successful because we will no longer have my income. We both know that God's perfect love casts out fear, but we don't know the next steps. I try not to make decisions in the heat of emotions anymore, but there are times when I feel like I am on a roller coaster of ups and downs waiting for it to come to a complete stop so I can see where the exit is.

For the first time in all of our discussions, we actually talked about what it would look like if I made that decision to leave this job, this career I've built, and stay in our home. In many ways I think I have been waiting to hear my husband say these words for almost four years. The funny thing is, when they were finally said, I stood like a deer in the headlights of an oncoming vehicle on I-75. The first thought that came to mind was, *I don't hate my job enough*, because walking away, even the right way, is a really big deal. Giving up the income, the title, the escape to my own little world where people work for me and listen to me just seems ludicrous, doesn't it? But then I look at my little people, these two little girls who have my blond hair and their daddy's long eyelashes, and I believe that I want to choose them. I find myself even more confused because is this a choice? For ten years I have been a working mama doing my best and giving my kids love and experiences and growing their faith by pouring into their lives. How do you ever know if that is enough?

Down the road, I hope my girls don't forget that I worked and had to leave them. I hope they remember that I gave it my all that I made mistakes but worked as unto the Lord. I want them to realize that through God I was able to climb a career ladder in remarkable time. I hope that they see all of that and it presses them to set their sights high, to dream big, and to work hard to get there. I also hope they know that there came a time in my life when I stood on the threshold of a different path and contemplated giving it all up to be more for them. And I could only come to this place because God opened new doors. He changed my husband's job, He changed our finances, He changed our circumstances, and then He began to change our hearts.

I am not sure what God has for my life. Maybe it is to let Him flow through every aspect of my soul while working this job, or perhaps He is calling me to go home and love my family. My story is unfinished, but my prayer for you is that through these pages of it you have found and will continue to find rest, comfort, and peace in knowing that He holds the pen to both yours and mine.

You might be wondering why I decided to write a book intended to encourage working mamas only to drop this final bombshell that I may not actually *want* to work anymore. I pray you don't see that as discouraging or disparaging in whatever circumstance you are in. I prayed over this chapter more than any other because I didn't want to hold anything back. God has given me this platform to share my story and to type out my testimony; to leave out this last piece would be dishonest and selling you short. I share this because maybe you are here, you were here, or you are going to be here. Maybe you are standing at the edge of decision and the fog is thick and you can't see your outstretched hand in front of you, and maybe knowing there's one other person in the world feeling this way at this moment feels a little bit like a hug. I wish this were interactive, because I sure could use one!

I am a planner without a plan. I know that if I run down this path to join the ranks of stay-at-home moms that God will take care of us. I know that He will provide as He always has. If that is not God's best for my life, though, I don't want to miss out on the blessings of my mission field. I also like to close the door on things quickly. I like to make up my mind and proceed with very little delay. It happens to be one of the defining traits of my personality on any of those standardized personality tests. But, this isn't the type of decision that you can rush into. There's too much at stake to make the wrong one, so I sit and I wait and I try to do what I have preached in this whole book: I pray. I will pray fervently, without ceasing, and rest in the promise that He knows the plans for my future. He knows them because He wrote them.

In two or five years from now when I'm ready to write the sequel, maybe then we will know the answer, what God decided to do next in my work life. There is no accident to His timing. There was no Chapter 10 until this past weekend, which does everything to confirm that you needed to read this as much as I needed to write it. If you are a mom and a wife and working for someone, you are likely tired, worn, and sometimes left wondering what all of this is for. Whether it's your closet, your car, or under your covers, you've had to find a place to cry those tears of exhaustion. You might feel at times like you could use a three-month nap, a refresh button, or a temporary exit hatch. We can load all the guilt on ourselves in one heaping pile because we think we are weak, or we can fall into our weakness, embrace it, and remember that in our weakness, He is the one who makes us strong. Maybe that season, the season I'm in, the season of losing one and starting another, and those series of bad days of being underappreciated are all part of His plan—a plan in which He allows the circumstances beyond our control so that there is no place to look but up. I am looking up. I am waiting on Him, and I am surrendering myself to His plan, all the while praying over each of you to do the same.

This gig is tough; this calling is not for the weak or faint-hearted. You have served, you have sacrificed, and you have embraced your mission field in a world that doesn't appreciate what we stand for, that doesn't encourage what we believe in, and that views our conflict between work and home as our greatest weakness. Success is defined for us, and comparison is the motivation. Everyone else has an opinion for our lives, and sometimes we wake up and realize that what we are actually doing with them is living another's dream. I laid out methods and practical tools in the book to help you start defining your own dream and fight what the world tells you. However, even with those methods we can find ourselves in seasons of waiting and uncertainty. There is hope for us both in the waiting. We can rest in the promise that one day we will stand before the King, daughters, real life princesses, and He will embrace us with arms wide open. But until that day comes . . .

This one's for you, the working mama!

Chapter 10 Application
Writing your Chapter 10

Dear Mama,

I just poured it all out there for you—every sad and sappy detail of being in one place and not knowing what's next. But the truth is, I wrote that four months before this moment in which I type this application section. I already know how that ended up working out, and I have never been more amazed at what God can do. I eagerly wait to share this with you in the next book, but that isn't what this is about. When I open this chapter and read it, which I've done about 100 times, I read the last sentence and I break out into full tears. I know what's coming; I wrote it! But it has the exact same effect of bringing out all the emotions I felt while writing it. That's because words are powerful. It takes me back to the raw emotion of that time when I needed to fully surrender to God the next step of my life. I am more grateful for the outcome because I can reflect on the journey.

You've endured ten chapters of my thoughts, God's word and applications. I'm hopeful that somewhere along the way just one phrase or paragraph sparked something. Whatever that is and whatever your current state is, sit here right now and write it down. Write your Chapter 10. Remind yourself where you are today, where you hope to be (because you now have a plan), and surrender it all to Him.

In four months—because that's exactly how long it took for me to see this happen—pull out your letter and see where God's brought you. Do it again in a year, three years, five years, and maybe even twenty years. He may not deliver on all of your requests because our plans often put limits on how big our God can be, but I'm certain you will find comfort in the words of your former self and glimpses of God's great love for you along the way.

My chapter 10, where I am today:

_____

_____

_____

_____

_____

_____

_____

_____

_____

_____

_____

_____

_____

Date:

Bonus Chapter

All the Single Mamas

He heals the brokenhearted and bandages their wounds.
Psalms 147:3

This one is for the mamas who are a little extra tired than the rest of us, who have to be strength and stability and security and love for more than just one. They are the ones who rarely get a break or a time-out. This is for the single mamas—the ladies who didn't ask for the hand this life dealt them but play it with all of their hearts because there really is no other choice. I can't pretend for a minute to know what life is like in your shoes, but I've been blessed and privileged to do life with a few women just like you. These are women who don't just take the lemons life gives them and make lemonade; they make it with a twist and one of those tiny, bright-colored paper umbrellas on top.

At fifteen years old, I walked into Chris's house for the first time as his girlfriend and met his mom. I loved her almost immediately. She was real. She was strong, independent, and loving. I wasn't just dating a boy back then; I was taking on his whole family. I spent more nights around their dinner table than I did my own some weeks. And so over the years this lady became my friend, my support, my encouragement, and my other mother. Vicki has her own story to tell. It's one of triumph, perseverance, and overcoming the odds as the ultimate single mama. She took on a life that probably wasn't what she'd envisioned, and she owned it. I admired her from day one because she went to work yet still came home every day and engaged with her kids, supported them in their activities, put a hot meal on the table, and took time to sit and talk and really listen. I watched her sacrifice of herself, her time, and her resources to give her kids the very best. There were days I just felt exhausted for her! Day in and day out with very little reprieve she persevered and pressed on toward the prize that God had for her.

For Vicki, look no further than her children if you are wondering how well her life was lived. We've already established that the one I married is pretty great, but he is one of three. Just basic odds would say that at least one of them should have some neck tattoos or a mug shot from a night of mistakes, but not among these three. They love the Lord and serve Him daily, they sacrifice for those in need, and they love their spouses fiercely. They didn't have the privilege of growing up with this love between parents modeled for them on a daily basis, yet along the way they picked up a value for family and appreciation for selfless love.

Your kids may be young and you may think that your situation is messing them up day after day, but one day, you might have a daughter-in-law who sits down to write a book and tells the world how you taught your son to love her well. You may have a daughter who runs a company or runs for president because you showed her that life is filled with challenges that don't need to get you down. Mama, give yourself a break. Love well and put Him first, and the rest will have a way of falling into place. Find your village, allow for support, and every once in a while you deserve (Yes, I said it! DESERVE!) a break.

In high school, every few months Chris and his siblings would either spend a few days visiting their dad in town or go for a couple of weeks to see him at his house. This was when I saw Vicki rest. This was when she allowed herself to sit on a beach with a book or get away with a friend to recharge her batteries. On one occasion when they were all away, she and I met for a regrettable blooming onion and a movie. She talked about how she missed her kids, and I knew it was genuine, but I could also see the benefit of some rest. There is no shame in needing to call a time-out, even if you don't have someone to take your kids for a week. You could take a day off while they are in school and grab a book and a chair and put your toes in some sand. It is good for the soul!

When Chris and I had just been married a few months, Vicki took a huge leap of faith and left her job of many years to become a partner in a new business. It was around this time when God took that fancy pen of His and started to change the trajectory of her story. Her kids were growing and self-sufficient, and the time had come for Him to work in big ways in her life. He took that business and grew it into something only He could. It wasn't just monetary gain and success that blossomed in this time, but a depth of faith that showed her that the God who had carried her all this time was not finished yet.

Each time I sit down to write a new chapter, I pray that it meets you where you are. That you, as the reader, can relate to what God puts on my heart and my mind and that in some way it's relevant. Maybe you glossed over some of my story because you don't have the support of a husband and your struggle is so much different. That's why this one's for you. If you do have a husband and decided to read this chapter, chances are you know a single mama. There's someone in your life that has a little extra struggle in her attempt at this parenting thing. Maybe God placed you in her life to be the person who shows up, who spends a few extra minutes to check in on her, or who doubles a dinner recipe and drops half off unannounced to give her a break. You can't walk a mile in her shoes, but perhaps you can be the person God uses today to give those shoes a little extra shine! Remember, we are all in this together on the same team. There is no offense or defense, and just because we have to do it a little differently doesn't mean we need to go at it alone.

This last bonus chapter is just an extra hug for the single mama. Thanks for hanging in there with my journey, even if it looks different than yours, and please find hope in the fact that all of the promises God made for my life apply to your own. God is good all of the time, even in the lows and the loneliness. I'm praying that you can find the unconditional love your heart seeks and build the community you need to pour into your life. You are not a charity case when your village reaches out to help. If that lie plagues you when someone offers to take your kids for the night or cook you a meal, I rebuke that for you! You are actually the princess God created you to be, and you are worthy and loved. The way He chooses to reiterate that to your heart may be through the loving acts of kindness demonstrated by His followers, your village.

If you are a single mama who is struggling, this story is not meant to create false hope and a belief that if you just follow certain steps success will find you. This story is to encourage you, because I know your struggle is real. Girl, I know that you are carrying a pressure and a weight for your family that you are not designed to carry alone. There is a calling on your life that you may not have asked for or dreamed you would be living, but God knew. He knew even before you were born what your life would look like. And He doesn't call the equipped to walk the tough paths; rather, He equips the called. I'm confident that someday you will look back on this life, and, if you've allowed Jesus to be at the center, to be the fountain you turn to when you thirst, you will see so many ways that God carried you.

This one's for you, the single mama.

Bonus Application
Love on a single mama

This week, I want you to think about one singe mama you know. Even if this is you, think about a friend in the same position. Now love that mama by thinking of one practical way that you can be the hands and feet of Jesus in her life. Choose one of the following, or come up with something on your own. But be obedient, because God calls us to serve others, and these mamas are a great place to start.

- Double your dinner recipe this week and drop off the extra unannounced. It's easy for the person to tell you no if you ask, but if you show up with dinner that can be eaten that night or reheated the next; it is hard for her to turn you away.
- Send her flowers. Don't you just love to receive flowers out of the blue? I get it, this one takes money, but if you are an Amazon Prime user you can send flowers including delivery for $20–$30, and just think how much that will bless her.
- Offer to watch her kids. Invite her kids over for an evening or sleepover or offer to go over one night and watch them in her home. This requires your time, which is often our most valuable resource. But think of how God can return your time and bless this mama.
- Invite her to church with you; bring her into your community.

Acknowledgments

God gave me the words, time, and resources to bring this dream into reality, but I believe He had some help in the execution:

For my husband, Chris: You are the love of my life (literally), and without your belief in me and pushing me to finish, I would have given up on this 100 times over. This book exists because you told me I could do it, you supported the project in every way, and you gave me the tough love I needed in reminding me nothing worth it is ever without opposition.

Ella and Meadow, there would not be a "working mama" without the kids who gave me the title. You are the lights of my life, and I am so thankful for the wild ride of parenting you both that has allowed me to experience all of the joys and emotions wrapped in these pages.

To my mom, who was the best working mama I have ever known: You set the bar high and showed me how this is done.

And to my dad, who packed my lunches every day: You gave me my sense of humor and always believed in my potential.

To my village: Bible Babes (Debbie, Chris, Connie, and Sherry), you are my weekly breath of fresh air and the family I get to choose. Monday night life group ladies (Dayna, Cassie, Lori, Haylie, Bre, and Becky) and their men, our life is better lived with you in it. Colleen, you showed me selfless love and sacrifice, and you are constantly the hands and feet of Jesus in my life. Brandon, you are my brother from another mother, and I am grateful for your love and support. My work sisters, you've supported me not only in the job but also in a big way in my writing of this story. Jamie B., thank you for showing up, not just that day when I needed you most but every day after that. Susan, thank you for making it easier for me to go off to work. And Mackenzie, thank you for giving us date nights.

For Noelle: Thank you for showing me that we are all on the same team and providing the beautiful, raw, and natural photos that bring this story to life.

And last but not least, for my mother-in-law, Vicki: You gave me the man of my dreams, and you have loved me as your own for twenty years. Your story will touch other single mamas. Thank you for letting me share a small piece of it.